"WOMAN," JESUS TOLD HER, "YOUR FAITH IS LARGE, AND YOUR REQUEST IS GRANTED." AND HER DAUGHTER WAS HEALED RIGHT THEN.

(Matthew 15:28 TLB)

BELIEVE
BIG

MARILYN HICKEY'S
COMPLETE GUIDE TO FAITH

BY: MARILYN HICKEY

TABLE OF CONTENTS

INTRODUCTION

Dear Friend,

Often, when we are experiencing hard times, people will encourage us to "just have faith." That's good advice—if we understand what faith really is. Some think that having faith means sitting back and doing nothing, but true faith is alive and active.

Developing an active faith—that gets results—is a journey, and I have written *Believe Big: Marilyn Hickey's Complete Guide to Faith* as a guidebook to lead you on that path. I am thrilled that you have chosen to walk this road with me to a more dynamic and rewarding faith, and I know you will be greatly blessed with each step you take.

God has given us the *"measure of faith"* (Romans 12:3) to sustain us: *"Now faith is the assurance of things hoped for, the conviction of things not seen"* (Hebrews 11:1). To have faith in God, we must believe in and believe for things we cannot see. This can be very difficult when we are surrounded and even overwhelmed by the visible world pressing in from all sides—demanding our attention.

The enemy would have us believe only in the troubles of this world, but true faith is living successfully in the visible world by trusting in the goodness of a God we cannot see. This world can weaken, even defeat us; faith gives us vitality and victory. Throughout the chapters of this book, you will find stories of real people whose faith carried them through seemingly impossible circumstances. Your faith can do the same for you!

Here, you will find the secrets to building a strong and active faith. You will learn the definition, fundamentals, and sources of an enduring faith. You will also learn how to guard against the greatest destroyers of faith including your own tongue. Discover how faith can overcome your trials and help you get answers to your prayers. See faith in action in the lives of some well-known (and not-so-well-known) heroes and heroines in the Bible.

This book springs from my prayer for you to experience the joy of living out a vigorous faith in all aspects of your life. I believe that as you read and practice the action plans at the end of each chapter, your faith will grow and grow, and you will be rewarded with confidence and prosperity. Burdens will be lighter, fears will evaporate, and *your every need will be met.*

In His love and mine,

1

DISCOVER FAITH—
THE UNSEEN REALM

Now faith is the assurance of things hoped for
the conviction of things not seen. (Hebrews 11:1)

To fully understand faith, you must realize that the world you can't see (the invisible) is as real as the one you can see (the visible). You can't see oxygen, but you breathe it for life—it is vital to our existence. How silly it would be to say that oxygen doesn't exist just because you can't see it. The invisible is given form and substance by your faith: *"For we walk by faith, not by sight"* (2 Corinthians 5:7).

God will reveal a truth from His Word, but you may not see an immediate, physical manifestation of it! This doesn't mean that His Word is false; it only means that we are not able to see the truth *with our eyes* or recognize it *with our senses.* When you put your trust in God, you believe in something you can't touch or see:

> *While we look not at the things which are seen, but at the things which are not seen: for the things which are seen are temporal; but the things which are not seen are eternal.*
> (2 Corinthians 4:18 KJV)

Faith is vital to your life; without it, you can't please God. You may truly want to please God and be like Him yet feel that you can't pull one more ounce of faith out of the hat! Let's be honest—we aren't capable of producing God-pleasing faith in our own strength. In order to please Him and be like Him, we must have His kind of faith, not faith built on our level of education, how much money we make, or how holy we appear to be:

> *But without faith it is impossible to please him: for he that cometh to God must believe that he is, and that he is a rewarder of them that diligently seek him.*
> (Hebrews 11:6 KJV)

How can you grasp and gain this special faith for your own life? You must go to God's Word to learn what God-kind-of-faith is and how to attain it:

> *But my righteous one shall live by faith; and if he shrinks back, my soul has no pleasure in Him.* (Hebrews 10:38)

FAITH IS...

Webster's dictionary says faith is:

- Allegiance to duty or a person: LOYALTY
- Fidelity to one's promises
- Belief and trust in and loyalty to God
- Firm belief in something for which there is no proof
- A system of religious beliefs

You Can't Cope Without Hope

Now faith is the assurance of things hoped for,
the conviction of things not seen. (Hebrews 11:1)

A closer look at the classical definition of faith found in Hebrews shows us two major components: first, the assurance (or confirmation) of things hoped for; second, the proof or evidence of what we cannot see.

Hope is more than wishful thinking—it is the *vision in faith* of your *desire.* It is true that hoping cannot make something happen, but when hope is joined with your faith—and intertwined as partners—hope and faith are very powerful.

One good definition of hope is "to anticipate, usually with pleasure and confidence." Faith will feed hope and cause you to take the actions necessary to bring to pass the things hoped for.

What are you hoping and needing faith for? You may have a need for finances, a desire for healing, or resolution of a difficult circumstance. You can cultivate your faith by first, keeping the hope—your desire—in front of you; and secondly, continuously exercising your faith by acting like God's Word is true and real, even if you cannot see the results. Say, "I have it, although I can't see it, because *I know God's Word is true and He cannot lie.*"

Hope is a good thing—we need hope! Faith gives substance to the thing(s) *hoped for,* and we can be sure that our hope will not be disappointed if it is in God. If we have hope, we can cope with anything the devil sends our way.

Sometimes we have to keep on hoping even though it looks like all hope is gone. This was certainly the case with Abraham as he and Sarah were awaiting the birth of their promised son, Isaac:

> *In hope against hope he believed, so that he might become a father of many nations according to that which had been spoken, "So shall your descendants be."* (Romans 4:18)

If Abraham's faith had been based solely upon his circumstances, his hope probably would have been shattered. However, Abraham's hope was in God—and he received his promise!

The Word—Breakfast of Champions

You may be thinking, "Marilyn, hope is either there or it isn't. I can't just manufacture it." It's true that you can't create hope, but God's Word can! By feeding on His Word daily we can become saturated in the Word, and God's Word develops hope:

> *But we do [strongly and earnestly] desire for each of you to show the same diligence and sincerity [all the way through]*

in realizing and enjoying the full assurance and development of [your] hope until the end. (Hebrews 6:11 AMPC)

The more Word you receive into your spirit, the more your hope will grow, and the greater your faith will be.

Hatching Your Faith

In his book, *The Fourth Dimension*, Dr. David Yonggi Cho says faith goes through an incubation period before the answer can be seen or felt. He uses the word "incubation" to describe waiting, such as "sitting on (eggs) to hatch" or "causing something to develop (such as an idea)."

First, visualize a clear-cut picture of the objective of your faith. As you meditate on God's Word, visualize your objective coming to pass. If you are meditating on healing, visualize your body well. Get a clear-cut picture in mind—and be specific!

Dr. Cho recounts that during his early ministry, he was without a desk, a chair, and a bicycle—so He asked the Lord for them. He expected these items to arrive at any time; however, one, two, three, six months passed, and nothing happened. Since he felt the responsibility to be an example of faith for those around him, he became discouraged.

Dr. Cho cried out: "What's wrong, Lord?" God spoke and told him to be more specific in his requests; he had not expressed a clear-cut vision. He immediately spelled out his request to the Lord, "Please, Lord, send me a Philippine mahogany desk (of a certain size), an

Put in your heart the assurance of the answer!

iron-frame chair with rollers, and an American-made bicycle." The Lord quickened a scripture in his heart to help him maintain his faith until he received his answer: *"God . . . calleth those things which be not as though they were"* (Romans 4:17 KJV).

Dr. Cho explained to his congregation that just as a baby is in the mother's womb nine months before its birth, so he had "conceived" a desk, a chair, and a bicycle, and soon he received exactly what he had requested.

Second, you must have a burning desire for the thing you request. God rewards the earnest seeker, not the casual inquirer. You can't be laid-back and nonchalant in your requests and expect to get answers. Red-hot desire gets results: *"Delight yourself in the Lord; and He will give you the desires of your heart"* (Psalm 37:4).

Third, pray for assurance of the answer. Since faith is the "assurance of things hoped for," you need to put in your heart the assurance of the answer. Your assurance, or guarantee, is like the title deed to "the thing hoped for."

Finally, speak the Word into your situation. Speak the Word during the "incubation period"—and speak it boldly!

When Joshua and Caleb returned from spying out the land of Canaan, they spoke boldly about what they believed. Remember they were in the minority, but they did not allow themselves to be influenced by others.

They declared their faith. Faith in your heart is not enough—faith must be released by your mouth: *"The word is near you, in your mouth and in your heart"* (Romans 10:8 NKJV).

What Type of Faith are You Using?

Let's look at some different kinds of faith. Maybe you know someone who operates in one of the types of faith described below.

Human Faith

Even unbelievers talk about faith—faith that their business will succeed, faith in their mates or family, faith in their career efforts, or faith in their doctors. This is human faith that works for some people in natural ways. They believe in human achievements and many times attain them.

Religious Faith

People who believe in a creed, an organization, or a church, may look and sound good, but their faith is in what they are doing—man-made ordinances, rituals, or an order of service.

Experiential Faith

By his own admission, the faith of the Apostle Thomas was based on what he could see and touch:

> *The other disciples therefore said unto him, We have seen the LORD. But he said unto them, Except I shall see in his hands the print of the nails, and put my finger into the print of the nails, and thrust my hand into his side, I will not believe.* (John 20:25 KJV)

Many people today are just like Thomas, believing only what they can prove with their senses, what they experience.

Intellectual Faith

Giving mental assent to the idea of faith without putting your heart in it is merely "intellectual faith." This type of faith will not cause anything to change. The rich young ruler believed the right things and lived a good life, but he was not willing to involve his heart, make Jesus the Lord of his life, and follow and obey Him (see Luke 18:18–25).

Temporary Faith

This is the rocky ground in the parable of the "sower and the seed." Many hear the Word and receive it joyfully, but later they doubt and let their faith slip away:

> *"The one on whom seed was sown on the rocky places, this is the man who hears the word and immediately receives it with joy; yet he has no firm root in himself, but is only temporary, and when affliction or persecution arises because of the word, immediately he falls away."*
> (Matthew 13:20–21)

Revelation Faith

This kind of faith is the result of God's Word being illuminated by the Holy Spirit. It is a gift from Him. We can believe and act on it without confirmation or proof. Revelation faith affects the visible world, but it comes from the invisible one.

Revelation faith is the good ground in the parable of the sower and the seed: "For by grace you have been saved through faith; and that not of yourselves, it is the gift of God" (Ephesians 2:8). This faith expects the miracle-working power of God to operate;

therefore, it is not surprised when miracles happen!

Revelation faith is powerful; it commands the situation. We see this kind of faith in Jesus when He commanded winds to obey, diseases to flee, and the dead to be raised. This faith is amazingly creative; God used it to create the worlds:

> *By faith we understand that the worlds were prepared by the word of God, so that what is seen was not made out of things which are visible.* (Hebrews 11:3)

Who Is Your Foundation?

God, your heavenly Father, the Creator and Ruler of the universe, is the Author of your faith. He created everything, including human beings, and in doing so, *He chose you* to be His own. *"You did not choose Me, but I chose you . . ."* (John 15:16).

God has wonderful plans for you—His chosen creation—and He wants you to grow in maturity and wisdom. Because He loves you, He makes all things work together for your good! Of course, because the world is dominated by sin and Satan, bad things happen, but God takes care of His own:

> *And we know that God causes all things to work together for good to those who love God, to those who are called according to His purpose.* (Romans 8:28)

How can you have faith that God loves you and will always take care of you? Look at what the Word says about Him: God is all-powerful, all-knowing, always present, just, faithful, and true. He is *worthy* of your trust.

God Is Supreme

When I say that God is "supreme," I mean that He is "the best, the greatest, the utmost!" We have all heard God referred to as *omnipotent*, or "having all power." He also has other descriptions and attributes, such as *omniscient*, "knowing all things." God is certainly aware of everything that happens to you and me.

God is also *omnipresent*, "present in all places at all times," always close to you. God is just, doing only what is right. He can never be accused of evil or unfairness.

This is the God in whom you can trust! He is the foundation of your faith, the one who will never fail you: *"For nothing will be impossible with God"* (Luke 1:37).

God Keeps His Word

We can trust God to mean what He says and to carry out what He promises. He keeps His Word and the Word will accomplish what it is sent to do:

> *So will My word be which goes forth from My mouth; it will not return to Me empty, without accomplishing what I desire, and without succeeding in the matter for which I sent it.*
> (Isaiah 55:11)

Your faith is based on the promises of God, a God who has shown Himself to be totally reliable. Your faith is not "blind"; you can rely on the one who is righteous, trustworthy, and faithful.

God Is Faithful

God, Himself, operates by faith, and as His child you should imitate Him: *"The just shall live by his faith"* (Habakkuk 2:4 KJV). God desires for us to be full of faith because His very character is faithfulness: *"If we are faithless, He remains faithful, for He cannot deny Himself"* (2 Timothy 2:13).

An exciting aspect of God's faithfulness is that when you walk in the truth of His Word, He will watch over your children and your children's children!

Know therefore that the LORD your God, He is God, the faithful God, who keeps His covenant and His loving kindness to a thousandth generation with those who love Him and keep His commandments. (Deuteronomy 7:9)

A Covenant for Your Family

My family is my priority; when I travel, I think of them often. It is easy to worry: "How are they doing? Are they all right?" However, I bring my mind back into line, "Wait a minute! Early this morning I spoke God's Word into every situation at home and I rest in that."

The Word of God will not let you down! The Word will work in your situation. The Word is the most powerful thing in the world. If God can hold up the world, He can take care of my loved ones and yours.

This truth was demonstrated in a dramatic way when our daughter Sarah was in kindergarten. The church had arranged a special luncheon for ladies and great care had been taken to plan the event well. As the pastor's wife, I had to be there, but normally I picked Sarah up at the bus stop at that time. So, I asked a woman from our church to meet Sarah for me. I gave the woman specific, detailed directions about where Sarah would get off the bus.

I repeated the instructions so they would be clear and put my mind at rest so I could concentrate on the luncheon. Eighteen hundred people attended, and many souls were saved. People even got saved out in the parking lot! It was a wonderful, victorious day.

In the meantime, five-year-old Sarah had an adventure! She got off her bus, looked around for someone to meet her, then sat down on the grass and waited—and waited and waited. The woman who was to meet her had gotten the directions confused and was waiting two blocks away. She waited for an hour, then panicked and returned to the church.

Sarah remembered to pray. "God, I need to get home, so you show me how to go. Thank you, God."

Near our house was a canal that Sarah had to cross to get home. She didn't want to get her shoes muddy, so she prayed again, "Dear God, please show me how to cross the canal so I won't get my feet wet and muddy." She told us the Lord led her to a place where there were rocks and she could cross the canal safely "on dry land."

Her next hurdle was getting inside the house. We had put an "emergency key" in a safe place that she could reach. She found it, but she had never unlocked the door by herself. However, she was able to let herself in the house, where she called the church office, and reached my administrative assistant.

"Sarah, where are you? Are you all right?"

Sarah told her she was at home and my administrative assistant quickly went and picked her up. So, all ended well.

God's Faithfulness to Us

Forever, O LORD, *Your word is settled in heaven. Your **faithfulness** continues throughout all generations; You established the earth, and it stands.* (Psalm 119:89–90)

The LORD's *loving kindnesses indeed never cease, for His compassions never fail. They are new every morning; great is Your **faithfulness**.* (Lamentations 3:22–23)

*God is **faithful**, through whom you were called into fellowship with His Son, Jesus Christ our Lord.* (1 Corinthians 1:9)

***Faithful** is He who calls you, and He also will bring it to pass.* (1 Thessalonians 5:24)

However, it hadn't yet ended for me. "God, this is terrible, absolutely terrible! I'm never going to do this kind of thing again. I can't be running around trying to have a big event when my children need me. Never again!"

The Lord spoke very directly to me, "Isn't Sarah all right?"

"Yes, Lord, she is."

"Did I take care of her?"

"Yes, Lord, you did."

I suddenly knew where He was going with this. "When you're about my business, I'm about your business." That does not mean that if I neglect my family, He will intervene, but God is faithful when we are faithful. There are countless scriptures that describe God's undeniable and unquestionable faithfulness, His total reliability. You can count on God!

A Lifetime Guarantee!

Our heavenly Father guarantees His promise by swearing upon His own integrity:

For when God made the promise to Abraham, since He could swear by no one greater, He swore by Himself. (Hebrews 6:13)

God's Word is full of promises to touch every part of your life: *"Forever, O LORD, Your word is settled in heaven"* (Psalm 119:89). His Word endures, and it will never pass away. *"The grass withers, the flower fades, but the word of our God stands forever"* (Isaiah 40:8).

"And as for Me, this is My covenant with them," says the LORD: "My Spirit which is upon you, and My words which I have put in your mouth shall not depart from your mouth, nor from the mouth of your offspring, nor from the mouth of your offspring's offspring," says the LORD, "from now and forever." (Isaiah 59:21)

We can fail to realize the significance of speaking faith-filled words in front of our children—the next generation. One evening when Sarah and I were driving home from church, I said something really negative.

Sarah corrected me: "Mother, watch the words of your mouth; you know you'll get what you say!"

God pledges His Word is valid and true: *"As for God, His way is blameless; the word of the LORD is tested"* (2 Samuel 22:31). God's Word is refined and pure as gold. When you read the Word, you never have to wonder if it has been watered down:

> *The words of the LORD are pure words; as silver tried in a furnace on the earth, refined seven times.* (Psalm 12:6)

God's Word is righteous: *"For the word of the LORD is upright; and all His work is done in faithfulness"* (Psalm 33:4). The Word is truth and the promises of God were confirmed in Christ Jesus: *"Sanctify them in the truth; Your word is truth"* (John 17:17).

Jesus went about healing all who were sick, so we know that God's Word has healing power: *"He sent His word and healed them, and delivered them from their destructions"* (Psalm 107:20).

Whatever struggle you are in, whether it be grief, stress, financial, or physical problems, the promises of the Word are your strength: *"My soul weeps because of grief; strengthen me according to Your word"* (Psalm 119:28). When you need light and understanding, wisdom and guidance, turn to His Word: *"The unfolding of Your words gives light; it gives understanding to the simple"* (Psalm 119:130).

God's Word brings salvation and then becomes your textbook for life. That is why it is vitally important to know the Word—its promises—and to understand they belong to you, now:

But these have been written so that you may believe that Jesus is the Christ, the Son of God; and that believing you may have life in His name. (John 20:31)

Just hearing or reading the Word is not enough; you must meditate on it and let the Holy Spirit make it real so that you can apply it to your life. Many people, even unbelievers, know something about the Word of God, but they don't know the *power* of His Word and how it can change their lives.

The Word of God brings forth fruit in your life, whether you realize it or not. It is impossible for God's Word to lie dormant, inactive, and unproductive. When you plant seeds in good soil in your garden—water, fertilize, and carefully tend the garden—it will bear fruit! This is a law of nature, and a law of God:

And the one on whom seed was sown on the good soil, this is the man who hears the word and understands it; who indeed bears fruit. (Matthew 13:23)

Our heavenly Father says, "Yes," to His promises. When you rely on the Word of God, He will honor it. Doesn't that give you peace and confidence? When your confidence is in Him, He will reward your trust:

For as many as are the promises of God, in Him they are yes; therefore also through Him is our Amen to the glory of God through us. (2 Corinthians 1:20)

As you begin to "personalize" the Word by reading, meditating, and speaking it, the character of Christ begins to develop in you:

For by these He has granted to us His precious and magnificent promises, so that by them you may become partakers of the divine nature. (2 Peter 1:4)

How do God's promises affect our study on faith? The Word must be mixed with faith to operate in our lives. The power is in the Word, but it's *activated* by your faith:

For indeed we have had good news preached to us, just as they also; but the word they heard did not profit them, because it was not united by faith in those who heard. (Hebrews 4:2)

Remember it was through faith that Abraham and Sarah received God's promise:

For the promise to Abraham or to his descendants that he would be heir of the world was not through the Law, but through the righteousness of faith. (Romans 4:13)

Even Jesus, the Son of God, could not use the healing promises of God where there was not an atmosphere of faith and belief:

And He was not able to do even one work of power there, except that He laid His hands on a few sickly people [and] cured them. And He marveled because of their unbelief (their lack of faith in Him). (Mark 6:5–6 AMPC)

THE PROMISES OF GOD

HIS WORD ENDURES

"Heaven and earth will pass away, but My words will not pass away." (Matthew 24:35)

HIS WORD IS VALID

Every word of God is tested; He is a shield to those who take refuge in Him. (Proverbs 30:5)

HIS WORD IS POWERFUL

"For with God nothing is ever impossible and no word from God shall be without power or impossible of fulfillment." (Luke 1:37 AMPC)

HIS WORD IS FOR YOU NOW

My son, observe the commandment of your father and do not forsake the teaching of your mother; bind them continually on your heart; tie them around your neck. When you walk about, they will guide you; When you sleep, they will watch over you; and when you awake, they will talk to you. For the commandment is a lamp, and the teaching is light; and reproofs for discipline are the wayof life. (Proverbs 6:20–23)

HIS PROMISES ARE CONDITIONAL

For indeed we have had good news preached to us, just as they also; but the word they heard did not profit them, because it was not united by faith in those who heard. (Hebrews 4:2)

Walk Your Talk

Faith without works is useless because if we talk about our faith, but don't act on what we believe, nothing is accomplished. *"Even so faith, if it hath not works, is dead, being alone"* (James 2:17 KJV).

Rahab, the harlot, is a perfect example of someone who heard the Word of the Lord, accepted God to be the Lord of heaven and earth, then followed through with her actions. She heard a rumor about the things God had done for the Israelites, and she knew she had to take action:

> *But the woman* [Rahab] *had taken the two men* [the spies] *and hidden them…* [And she spoke to them:] *Now then, I pray you, swear to me by the Lord, since I have shown you kindness, that you also will show kindness to my father's house, and give me a sure sign, And save alive my father and mother, my brothers and sisters, and all they have, and deliver us from death.*
> (Joshua 2:4, 12–13 AMPC)

Rahab was concerned not only with her own safety, but that of her immediate family. She pleaded that they also be spared when the Israelites took the city. Before the spies left, they helped her devise a plan. They told her to gather her family in her house and hang a scarlet cord from her window as a marker, and that red cord became her hope! She hung the cord out the window knowing that the situation was not hopeless for her and her family.

Rahab put her hope in her newfound God, and the action she took, coupled with her faith, resulted in the salvation of her entire household. As an added blessing, she married an Israelite and became a "blessed one." Rahab had a son named Boaz who was an ancestor in the lineage of David and the Lord Jesus Christ. Faith plus action will put you over!

Undeniably, the Word of God demonstrates that, without action, faith—and the promises—lie dormant. If we are believers, then we believe—and our actions reflect our trust.

When physical evidence is lacking, press on. When your faith is in the "incubation" period, continue to patiently nurture its seed, and you will reap the promised harvest. Continue to walk, talk, and live by faith—no matter if you see anything happening or not—knowing that the foundation of your faith, God Himself, is infinitely trustworthy.

STEPS TO BELIEVING BIG

1.

Write down examples of when your faith
may have been categorized as:

Human_____

_____

_____

Religious_____

_____

_____

Experiential_____

_____

_____

Intellectual_____

_____

_____

Temporary_____

_____

_____

Revelation_____

_____

_____

2.

After you have searched the Word for promises
concerning your situation, fuse your hope with
faith! Share your hope with another person.

3.

If you have been praying for a long time for something
and haven't seen the answer, apply God's Word
to the situation until you see it change!

4.

Ask God to help you speak only positive, faith-filled
words. Record these words in a journal or notebook.

_____

_____

_____

_____

5.

List some of God's promises and ask Him to help you understand their place in your personal "faith walk."

_____

_____

_____

_____

_____

2

THE GIFT THAT KEEPS ON GIVING

…God hath dealt to every man the measure
of faith. (Romans 12:3 KJV)

D o you ever wonder if you have enough faith to get what the Bible says you have coming from God? At times, does it seem like you have very little or no faith at all? Have you ever tried to believe God for something, but didn't get any results? I have great news! Regardless of how faith-less you feel or how spiritually unsuccessful you've been, *you do have faith!* In fact, you have enough faith to get everything God has for you and more.

Do you think that any "great" person of faith acquired a huge amount right up front? No! First, they received a little bit of faith, then it went through normal growth patterns, matured, and later reached a state of greatness. When we read about the people of great faith in "The Faith Hall of Fame" in Hebrews 11, do we read any of the mistakes these people made? No! Only good things are related, but surely, they didn't come into perfect faith without erring in some way.

It used to bother me that God told us only about the mighty exploits of Abel, Enoch, Noah, Abraham, Sarah, and the others in Hebrews 11 without sharing any of their failures. "God, you're not telling us the whole story—you only tell about their faith." God dealt with me and spoke very clearly, "That's right, because I have forgotten everything they repented of." The same is true for you—He has forgiven everything you've repented of because it's His will to forget it. What God remembers about you is your faith, because faith pleases Him. Isn't it wonderful that God forgets about our sins and remembers our faith?

The Nature of Faith

You may have a desire for more faith but wonder how to get it. The only way you can continually move in faith is to *become a man or woman of the Word*—that is the only way faith can come: *"Faith comes by hearing, and hearing by the word of God"* (Romans 10:17 NKJV). The closer you get to Jesus and the more you really know Him, the more your faith will grow.

How do you get to know Him better? Learn His Word! As you see what He teaches about life situations and make Him your faith source, you will be able to walk through all circumstances confident in Him. If you make Jesus the focal point of your faith walk, He will mature and perfect your faith. The Holy Spirit gives our

human spirits understanding and will help our minds compre-
hend the Word:

Looking away [from all that will distract] to Jesus, Who is the
Leader and the Source of our faith [giving the first incentive to
our belief] and is also its Finisher, [bringing it to maturity and
perfection]. (Hebrews 12:2 AMPC)

Being born of God makes you a child of God, so your new
nature is a *faith* nature. The child has the nature of the parents;
since God is a faith God, it is normal that His children have His
kind of faith. *"And Jesus answered saying to them, 'Have faith in*
God'" (Mark 11:22). Some scholars translate this as, "Have the
God-kind of faith." It is God's will and pleasure that we move in
His kind of powerful, mountain-moving faith:

By faith we understand that the worlds were prepared by the
word of God, so that what is seen was not made out of things
which are visible. (Hebrews 11:3)

A Special Gift

To another faith by the same Spirit, to another gifts of healing by
the one Spirit. (1 Corinthians 12:9)

Sometimes the Holy Spirit will drop a special "gift of faith" into
your spirit for a specific task. You might long to see a person saved,
someone healed or delivered, or some other need met, and by this

"gift of faith" you will know for sure that the thing will come to pass. There will be no room for doubt.

I believe Queen Esther operated in this kind of "revelation faith" when she spoke out boldly and rescued her people. A paraphrase of Esther 4:16 has her saying, "If I perish, I perish, but I'm going to get my people free." Did she have fear? I believe she did, but she overcame her fear and became bold because she had heard from God.

The Inner Journey of Faith

Vine's Expository Dictionary defines the heart as "the chief organ of physical life." *"For the life of the flesh is in the blood"* (Leviticus 17:11). The word "heart" came to stand for man's entire mental and moral activity, both the rational and the emotional elements. The heart occupies the most important place in the human system and is used figuratively for the personal life.

We see over and over again that faith comes through your heart or your spirit, rather than through the senses. In 1 Peter 3:4, the spirit is called *"the hidden person of the heart."* In Romans 7:22, it is called *"the inner man."* It is shown to be the part of you that believes, the part of you where faith takes place: *"For with the heart a person believes..."* (Romans 10:10 AMPC). This part of your being is re-created and renewed daily:

Therefore we do not lose heart, but though our outer man is decaying, yet our inner man is being renewed day by day.
(2 Corinthians 4:16)

That He would grant you, according to the riches of His glory, to be strengthened with power through His Spirit in the inner man. (Ephesians 3:16)

There are times when your mind cannot grasp God's truth, but your heart or spirit is receiving it. In fact, many times our minds can actually hinder us! Thankfully, the Holy Spirit helps your mind understand what your heart readily receives from God:

For to us God revealed them through the Spirit; for the Spirit searches all things, even the depths of God. But a natural man does not accept the things of the Spirit of God, for they are foolishness to him; and he cannot understand them, because they are spiritually appraised.
(1 Corinthians 2:10, 14)

But when He, the Spirit of truth, comes, He will guide you into all the truth; for He will not speak on His own initiative, but whatever He hears, He will speak; and He will disclose to you what is to come. (John 16:13)

Faith grows as the Word feeds your spirit.

Let the Holy Spirit teach you through the Word, because as the Word feeds your spirit, your faith will grow. If you grew up on a farm, you may know that a cow chews its food, swallows it down into one of its two stomachs, then brings it back up and chews it some more. This is referred to as "chewing its cud" and it aids nutrition.

On the first "chew" the cow gets a certain amount of nutrition; then when it comes up again, it chews some more and gets more nutrition. In this same way we need to chew on the Word of God. To meditate is to masticate God's Word. By "chewing" on the Word of God, I mean that when you read the Word over and over, you will almost always have something new revealed to you by the Holy Spirit. He is teaching you and feeding your spirit.

Faith Comes by . . . ?

So faith comes from hearing, and hearing
by the word of Christ. (Romans 10:17)

You and I need to make a commitment to spend a great deal of time in God's Word—every day. I know you're busy, you have jobs and family, and many demands on your life, but there are ways to conserve or "redeem" time. The word "redeem" means "to buy back or pay a ransom for," and that's exactly what you can do when your time is stolen.

The Word

Logos: The revealed will of God; a direct revelation given by Christ. The personal manifestation of the whole Deity.

Rhema: The individual scripture which the Spirit brings to our remembrance for us in time of need.

(Definitions from *Vine's Complete Expository Dictionary of Old and New Testament Words.*)

Arrange your daily schedule around the Word, because receiving God's Word into your spirit is the most important thing you can do. If you're cooking or ironing, or even taking a relaxing bath, listen to a recording of the New Testament. When you're running errands in your car, or commuting to work, always have a download on your phone or CD of the Bible with you and listen to it. You'll be surprised how much of the Word you can put in your spirit this way. Don't miss these opportunities to buy back time and grow in faith through the Word!

You can also "hear" the Word by making a habit of reading it *aloud*, whenever possible. This gives you double hearing—with your natural ear and your inner ear. You can hear by reading, listening, confessing, and meditating the Word.

The whole, revealed Word of God is called *logos*. The singular Word which God speaks to you for a specific situation is called *rhema*. When you fill your heart with the *logos*, you build a reserve from which the Holy Spirit can bring to your remembrance a specific *rhema* for your situation. As you speak *rhema* into the circumstances, you will see things change and your faith will grow.

You can use the Word to fight and defeat your foe, the devil. Don't feel that you need to bring the entire Bible against him—the Holy Spirit will bring to your remembrance a scripture for that exact time and need. That's why it is absolutely necessary to regularly store the Word in your mind, because the Spirit can't bring it to remembrance if it's not there! The sword of the Spirit referred to in the following scripture is a *rhema* of God, an individual word that will be like a sword against the enemy:

And take THE HELMET OF SALVATION, and the sword of the Spirit, which is the word of God. (Ephesians 6:17)

Jesus said that man is to live by the rhema of God—but it all starts with the *logos:*

But He answered and said, "It is written, 'MAN SHALL NOT LIVE ON BREAD ALONE, BUT ON EVERY WORD THAT PRODEEDS OUT OF THE MOUTH OF GOD.'" (Matthew 4:4)

The *logos* (the whole Word of God) forms the larger picture, but the guidance you receive on an everyday basis is through the *rhema* of God.

Rhema For Your Circumstances

"If you abide in Me, and My words abide in you, ask whatever you wish, and it shall be done for you." (John 15:7)

For the law of the Spirit of life in Christ Jesus has made me free from the law of sin and death. (Romans 8:2 NKJV)

He sent His word and healed them, and delivered them from their destructions. (Psalm 107:20 NKJV)

The young lions lack and suffer hunger; but those who seek the Lord shall not lack any good thing. (Psalm 34:10 NKJV)

Commit your works to the LORD, and your thoughts will be established. (Proverbs 16:3 NKJV)

"Behold, I give you the authority to trample on serpents and scorpions, and over all the power of the enemy, and nothing shall by any means hurt you." (Luke 10:19 NKJV)

Speak the Word

You cannot separate God from His Word. Become one with God's Word, because He watches over His Word as you confess it. God hears what you say, and *you also* hear what you say! You will believe what you constantly hear yourself saying; so keep saying what God says—the Word!

Jesus is actually called "The Word of God":

"He has a name written on him that no one knows but he himself. He is dressed in a robe dipped in blood, and his name is the Word of God." (Revelation 19:12–13 NIV)

When Sarah was in high school, she desperately wanted to be on the varsity basketball team, so she practiced and practiced.

At the same time, she began speaking words in faith, saying, "I'm on the varsity team this year in school. I'm going to be on the first-string varsity team." As she said the words, she believed them in her heart. She made the team and did well! She also had a desire to get good grades, so she began to speak words of faith in that area, as well: "I'm the head. I'm not the tail. I have the mind of Christ in me." Every morning before Sarah walked out the door to catch her bus, she'd say to me, "I'm ten times wiser! I'm wise because I have His wisdom."

When she got her report card, she had all A's except for one B! Speak and confess His Word into all areas of your life. Listen to yourself and discover what words you are speaking and loose the spirit of faith!

Turn Up the Volume

It is important to hear the Word, but it is more important that we *really listen* to what we hear—giving it our whole attention and attaching importance to it. Jesus specifically instructed us to be good listeners:

> *So take care how you listen; for whoever has, to him shall more be given; and whoever does not have, even what he thinks he has shall be taken away from him.* (Luke 8:18)

Jesus had just finished explaining the parable of the seed and the sower. (Read the entire parable in Luke 8:11–18.) The *"good soil"* heard the Word in an honest and good heart and held it fast. This was not passive hearing, but active listening with response! This is what made this soil successful and fruitful.

Isaac was deceived through his smell, taste, and feelings. When he heard the voice of Jacob, he should have heeded the voice—he should have listened to what he was hearing. Isaac heard the voice of Jacob, but allowed himself to be deceived:

> *Then Isaac said to Jacob, "Please come close, that I may feel you, my son, whether you are really my son Esau or not." So Jacob came close to Isaac his father, and he felt him and said, "The voice is the voice of Jacob, but the hands are the hands of Esau." He did not recognize him, because his hands were hairy like his brother Esau's hands; so he blessed him.* (Genesis 27:21–23)

The ability to *really* listen helped a woman get healed of a condition that she had suffered from for years. The woman with the issue of blood heard about Jesus and His healing power and gave action to what she heard. Her faith enabled her to move through the crowd and daringly touch the hem of His garment, even though her condition (by law) prohibited her from touching anyone:

> *And a certain woman, which had an issue of blood* [hemorrhage]
> *twelve years, ... When she had heard of Jesus, came in the press*
> *behind, and touched his garment.*
> (Mark 5:25, 27 KJV)

A spirit of faith was loosed in this woman and she said, "If I can touch His clothes, I will be healed." One translation from the Greek explains that she kept saying over and over, "I will be made whole. I will be made whole. I will be made whole." She had a single eye of faith and as she said it repeatedly, her faith was loosed. Her faith made her whole—and her faith came from really listening when she heard about Jesus.

We see a similar act of listening when Paul preached at Lystra and a lame man heard and responded. He accepted the words Paul said, then he heeded them, and faith came. Paul discerned faith in the man and said, "Stand upright on your feet!" and the man's faith resulted in total healing:

> *At Lystra there was sitting a certain man, without strength in*
> *his feet, lame from his mother's womb, who had never walked.*
> *This man was listening to Paul as he spoke, who, when he had*
> *fixed his gaze upon him and had seen that he had faith to*

be made well, said with a loud voice, "Stand upright on your feet." And he leaped up and began to walk. (Acts 14:8–10)

Planting the Word to Grow Your Faith

Memorize and personalize the following scriptures so that they will be in your spirit, then you can confess them for situations that arise:

The LORD is my shepherd, I shall not want. (Psalm 23:1)

"Do not fear, for I am with you; do not anxiously look about you, for I am your God. I will strengthen you, surely I will help you, surely I will uphold you with My righteous right hand." (Isaiah 41:10)

What then shall we say to these things? If God is for us, who is against us? (Romans 8:31)

I can do all things through Him who strengthens me. (Philippians 4:13)

The LORD is my light and my salvation; whom shall I fear? The LORD is the defense of my life; whom shall I dread? (Psalm 27:1)

And my God shall supply all your needs according to His riches in glory in Christ Jesus. (Philippians 4:19)

My help comes from the LORD, who made heaven and earth. (Psalm 121:2)

Meditate Day and Night

Much has been written and said about meditating, both in the secular and spiritual worlds. First, let's be clear on what we mean by "meditate" because the world uses the word in very ungodly ways. *Vine's Expository Dictionary* says that "meditate" means "ponder, imagine, attend to, practice, to care for." This is the same action as worry—only in reverse! Hearing the Word constantly is the best way for faith to come into your life.

> *Consequently, faith comes from hearing the message, and the message is heard through the word about Christ.*
> (Romans 10:17 NIV)

God has ordained meditation as a key means for us to constantly hear the Word. When we meditate, we go over and over a thought in our minds. We think it, we say it, then we think about it some more and that is how faith comes!

The best way to meditate is to memorize a portion of God's Word, then several times a day "meditate" or ponder it, say it over and over again, asking God to reveal truth from it. Personalize it—put the Word into your present situation, then visualize the Word coming to pass in your life. (Even when you are just reading the Word, personalize it, and you will discover that it will bring life and light to you.)

My late husband told a story about growing up near a relative, an elderly man, who would sit in his rocker on the front porch, rocking back and forth and repeating, "I wish I had a million dollars. I wish I had a million dollars. I wish I had a million dollars."

That old man made a lasting impression on my husband, and even as a young child he could see that wishing didn't get you what you wanted. Wishing to prosper will not make it happen; you need to learn God's Word then speak and act upon it!

Joshua faced a difficult task. It was his job to get the Israelites into the promised land, and he needed great faith in order to accomplish his assignment. God told him to have courage, but He also gave him specific instructions about meditating on the Word:

> *This book of the law shall not depart from your mouth, but you shall meditate on it day and night, so that you may be careful to do according to all that is written in it; for then you will make your way prosperous, and then you will have success. (Joshua 1:8)*

There are three keys to prosperity and success in this scripture: *speak* the Word (keep it in your mouth); *meditate* on the Word (keep it in your mind); and *obey* the Word (faith in action). Notice that the Lord told Joshua not to let the Word depart from his mouth. In other words, he was to speak it over and over again. Joshua obeyed, and he was able to lead Israel to victory:

> *How blessed is the man who does not walk in the counsel of the wicked, nor stand in the path of sinners, nor sit in the seat of scoffers! But his delight is in the law of the Lord, and in His law he meditates day and night. He will be like a tree firmly*

*planted by streams of water, which yields its fruit in its season,
and its leaf does not wither; and in whatever he does, he
prospers.* (Psalm 1:1–3)

There are marvelous promises for the righteous man in this
psalm who *meditates* on the Word day and night. The Word causes
him to be firmly planted, fruitful, and prosperous! It is the faiththat
comes from God's Word that will cause you to excel.

Sink Your Roots Deep

*Having been firmly rooted and now being built up in
Him and established in your faith, just as you were
instructed, and overflowing with gratitude.*
(Colossians 2:7)

It is essential that the faith you rely upon is your own. Do not
become dependent upon the personal faith of your pastor, teacher,
friend, or anyone else. God wants the faith which belongs to you,
to work for you. He wants you to be established in your own faith.

While we cannot make another's faith our own, we can learn
from the example of others. I learned about faith from my mother,
who was a mighty woman of the Word.

She became Spirit-filled when I was away at college; I came
home one weekend to find everything changed! Bibles were on
the end tables, our home had been transformed in many ways,
and my mother was like a different person, turned on for Jesus. I
didn't know anything about this "Spirit-filled" life and it was
rather confusing to me.

There was a large cottonwood tree in our yard and the neighbors had one, too. The trees were separated by just a fence. The trees were so close that they looked like one tree. And they were filled with nasty, hideous worms. It was like a plague. These worms would drop a little thread-like substance after they had eaten a leaf and they were not at all discriminating in where they dropped it. If you were under the trees, you'd get droppings in your hair, and if you walked on the ground under the trees, your feet would "squish" on the material. It was dreadful!

My mother wanted my father to spray our tree, but he felt it was too expensive. Also, he told her, "I know the neighbors are having their tree sprayed, but those worms have eggs, and they'll hatch and then there will be more worms. It's just money down the drain." Nothing could persuade him.

Mother was determined and she now had a new weapon in her arsenal: faith! "I'm going out there and curse those worms in the name of Jesus. They're on my tree on my property, and I'm going to tell them to get off, in Jesus's name."

I was horrified. "Mother, surely you're not going to do that in the daylight."

She was so bold! She walked out to our tree in the middle of the day, cursed those worms in the name of Jesus, and demanded that they *never* come back.

The next day we walked out into the backyard and it was really squishy. Not only were there droppings, but all the worms were on the ground, as well. They had fallen out of the tree—dead!

We watched the neighbor's tree and observed a very interesting thing. They sprayed, but the eggs still hatched, the worms came out again and continued to do their damage, just as Father had predicted. However, the worms from their tree never came over and bothered our tree. I believe they didn't dare cross over and touch our tree, because my mother had cursed them in the name of Jesus—and Jesus's name gives you dominion.

My mother spoke and "established" that our tree was protected by the name of Jesus. You can also establish a thing by speaking it out loud in agreement with God's Word. That's how you were saved: you believed, and you confessed Jesus as Lord. The word of faith should always be in your mouth:

> But what does it say? "THE WORD IS NEAR YOU, IN YOUR
> MOUTH AND IN YOUR HEART"—that is, the word of faith
> which we are preaching, that if you confess with your mouth
> Jesus is Lord, and believe in your heart that God raised Him
> from the dead, you shall be saved; for with the heart a person
> believes, resulting in righteousness, and with the mouth
> he confesses, resulting in salvation. (Romans 10:8–10)

When you confess the promises and blessings of God, you are claiming them as your own. You have been given a *"measure of faith,"* the *logos* of the Word, a will to choose, and a mouth to speak. The more you choose to speak the Word of God, the more it becomes yours and becomes a part of you; no one can take it from you.

Use It or Lose It

Once you have established your faith with God's Word, begin using it to receive the promises of God. Remember, His promises are obtained by faith:

Who by faith conquered kingdoms, performed acts of righteousness, obtained promises, shut the mouths of lions. (Hebrews 11:33)

God is faithful and He loves it when we use His Word to receive the promises of healing:

He Himself bore our sins in His body on the cross, so that we might die to sin and live to righteousness; for by His wounds you were healed. (1 Peter 2:24)

You may have a great desire to see members of your family saved. Rely on God's promises for their salvation:

They said, "Believe in the Lord Jesus, and you will be saved, you and your household." (Acts 16:31)

God's supply for your earthly needs is endless, and He is also able to provide all the wisdom you need to deal with life's situations:

And my God will supply all your needs according to His riches in glory in Christ Jesus. (Philippians 4:19)

But if any of you lacks wisdom, let him ask of God, who gives to all generously and without reproach, and it will be given to him. (James 1:5)

Have Bulldog Faith

You may have known the promises of God, confessed them, accepted them, and even received answers to some of your prayers; however, your faith can waver when you have confessed something for a long time and nothing has happened. What should you do? God wants you to *"hold fast to your confession."* Keep God's Word in the *"midst of your heart."* Be a bulldog; don't let go.

> *Therefore, since then we have a great high priest who has passed through the heavens, Jesus the Son of God, let us hold fast our confession.* (Hebrews 4:14)

> *My son, give attention to my words; incline your ear to my sayings. Do not let them depart from your sight; keep them in the midst of your heart. For they are life to those who find them and health to all their whole body.* (Proverbs 4:20–22)

Faith needs action, and expressing your faith is an indispensable means of communicating it. By speaking your faith, it will grow and multiply in your life and in the lives of others. If you share your doubts, they will multiply instead. Quit speaking your doubts. Don't let your words be more important than His words.

Love—Faith's Best Friend

No believer should seek to be a person of great faith without also seeking to love much, because *faith works by love.* In fact, it can't work without it. The Bible says that even if you have enough faith to move mountains, without love, you are nothing.

> *If I have the gift of prophecy, and know all mysteries and all knowledge; and if I have all faith, so as to remove mountains, but do not have love, I am nothing.* (1 Corinthians 13:2)

I have heard Kenneth Hagin, Jr. say, "If we are to live in line with God's Word, we must not only be the faith child of a faith God, but we must be the love child of a love God."

When Paul thanked God for the Thessalonians, he spoke of their *"work of faith"* and their *"labor of love"*—equally:

> *... Constantly bearing in mind your work of faith and labor of love and steadfastness of hope in our Lord Jesus Christ in the presence of our God and Father.*
> (1 Thessalonians 1:3)

Have you ever shared the gospel of Christ with a person and told him/her about the unspeakable love of Jesus? Talking about God's love can remind us again of how wonderful it is to know Him and make us want to please Him in everything we do. If you have an intimate relationship with Jesus and let His love live in you, you will have the kind of faith that can move mountains! Be a child of faith and love—equally—because our God is the author of both!

FAITH GROWS AS THE WORD FEEDS YOUR SPIRIT.

STEPS TO BELIEVING BIG

1.

Help your faith grow by doing
the following every day: Read the Word;
confess the Word; memorize the Word;
meditate on the Word; and obey the Word.

2.

Study the difference between the words logos and
rhema and explain them in your own words. Keep a
journal with the rhema words you hear from God.

3.

Ask the Lord to help you *personalize* your faith through
the Word. Follow the example of the following scripture:

He Himself bore our [my] *sins in His body on the cross,
so that we* [I] *might die to sin and live to righteousness;
for by His wounds you were [I was] healed.* (1 Peter 2:24)

4.

Meditate on how love affects faith by reading these verses:

Galatians 5:6–14
Ephesians 4:1–3
Ephesians 4:15, 29
Ephesians 5:1–2

5.

Think of a person of "great faith"
that you know. Write down a few spiritual habits
you could learn from them.

_____

_____

_____

_____

_____

_____

_____

_____

_____

_____

_____

_____

_____

_____

_____

3

THE VOCABULARY OF FAITH

By faith we understand that the worlds were prepared by the word of God, so that what is seen was not made out of things which are visible. (Hebrews 11:3)

Have you ever considered how much power there is in what you speak? Though it may not be visible to the naked eye like the immense force of the tumbling waters of Niagara Falls, there are tremendous positive and negative forces put to work when words are spoken out loud.

By the word of the LORD the heavens were made, and by the breath of His mouth all their host. For He spoke, and it was done; He commanded, and it stood fast. (Psalm 33:6, 9)

The book of Genesis reveals how God spoke the universe into existence; in fact, God released His faith through the creative power of His word ten times in the first chapter of Genesis. God's power is so awesome that all He had to do was speak and matter was created out of nothing: *"Then God said, 'Let there be light'; and there was light"* (Genesis 1:3). God said something and it was so:

> *"Let there be an expanse in the midst of the waters, and let it separate the waters from the waters."* (Genesis 1:6)

Further, He said, *"Let the earth sprout vegetation"* (Genesis 1:11), and it sprouted vegetation! Just like that—it was so. Can you imagine having the power to speak things into being? The universe and everything in it was created by God's spoken word. Even today, all things are sustained by that power:

> *And He is the radiance of His glory and the exact representation of His nature, and upholds all things by the word of His power.* (Hebrews 1:3)

Lucifer's Damning Declaration

> *"But you [Lucifer] said in your heart, 'I will ascend to heaven; I will raise my throne above the stars of God, and I will sit on the mount of assembly in the recesses of the north . . . I will make myself like the Most High.'"*
> (Isaiah 14:13–14)

Lucifer was a powerful and beautiful angel with a place of high honor in heaven. I believe he took the praise that came up from the earth and spoke that praise to God. One reason I believe this is because Lucifer had a beautiful voice; the Bible says his voice was like tambourines and pipes:

> . . . *The workmanship of your timbrels and pipes was prepared for you on the day you were created.*
> (Ezekiel 28:13 NKJV)

Lucifer was in a glorious position, but he didn't like being a servant—he didn't like his position or his image. So he tried to steal the praise that belonged to God. He became arrogant and exalted himself and wanted his own throne above God's.

Finally, God said, "That's enough!" and cast Lucifer out of heaven: *"How you have fallen from heaven, O star of the morning, son of the dawn!"* (Isaiah 14:12). Since that day, Satan has existed with only one purpose—to influence others to rebel against the Most High God. Every time Satan speaks, it is with lies and deceptions—his words have caused great damage and destruction.

Words That Set You Free

> *"'. . . The words that I speak to you are spirit, and they are life.' . . . Simon Peter answered Him, 'Lord, to whom shall we go? You have the words of eternal life.'"*
> (John 6:63, 68 NKJV)

Jesus's teachings give life and guidance and provide freedom. In the garden of Gethsemane, Jesus prayed to the Father, *"Thy will be done,"* and the Father led Him to the cross. On the cross, His last words were, *"It is finished,"* and those words are full of great meaning for us.

He gave His life that you might go free from the tyranny of sin. He gave His life that you might live. It is a "finished" work! The death and resurrection of Jesus Christ took power from the devil, and granted you new power:

> *I have been crucified with Christ; it is no longer I who live, but Christ lives in me; and the life which I now live in the flesh I live by faith in the Son of God, who loved me and gave Himself for me.* (Galatians 2:20 NKJV)

If you are born again, Christ lives in you. Therefore, when you speak His Word, you overrule the lies of Satan. Jesus's words bring overcoming power to every circumstance of your life.

Your Tongue Is a Weapon

> *So also the tongue is a small part of the body, and yet it boasts of great things. See how great a forest is set aflame by such a small fire!* (James 3:5)

The tongue is a powerful weapon for good or evil.

Few people truly realize their tongue is a powerful weapon. It is a mighty force in your life that can be used for good or evil. A bit in the mouth of a horse causes him to go in the right direction, and a rudder guides a ship. In the same way, your tongue has the power to guide your thoughts, emotions, and body into paths of prosperity and success.

On the negative side, your tongue can damage and destroy your physical body, thought life, and emotions and bring you to ruin. Corrupt words can destroy those about you and cause lasting pain and devastation:

> *There is one who speaks rashly like the thrusts of a sword, but the tongue of the wise brings healing.* (Proverbs 12:18)

Satan can use your negative words to defeat you. There is good news however; your words can defeat Satan! Revelation 12:11 says that God's children overcome Satan by *"the blood of the Lamb"* and *"the word of their testimony."* We overcome the wicked one by using our tongues against him—our powerful tongues!

Few, if any of us, get through life without having negative words spoken against us and our loved ones. You might wonder if the negative confessions of others can curse your life. God's Word in Isaiah 54:17 says, "No!"

> *"No weapon that is formed against you will prosper; and every tongue that accuses you in judgment you will condemn. This is the heritage of the servants of the Lord, and their vindication is from Me," declares the Lord.*

If something negative is said or you have been falsely accused, don't try to fight it in a natural way. Condemn the words spoken against you in the name of Jesus. Never condemn the *person*, only their *words*. Then negative words cannot harm you.

Words can comfort the sad, heal the brokenhearted, cool anger, and bring order to confusion. They can restore courage, calm the fearful, motivate right actions, and stop the wicked one. Words can heal the sick, release the imprisoned, and feed the poor. Speaking the right words will cause you to be satisfied with your life:

> *With the fruit of a man's mouth his stomach will be satisfied; he will be satisfied with the product of his lips.* (Proverbs 18:20)

Best and most beneficial of all, your words can announce God's Word! The words you speak can be more precious than gold and more valuable than jewels (see Proverbs 20:15).

> *Like apples of gold in settings of silver is a word spoken in right circumstances. Like an earring of gold and an ornament of fine gold is a wise reprover to a listening ear.* (Proverbs 25:11–12)

Recently, I was praying for a woman for the healing of her cancer. People would ask me how she was doing, and I would tell them that she wasn't doing very well. I said that three or four times.

The Lord said to me, "Don't say that. You don't have to say that she is not doing well. You can just say that the reports are not good, but we are believing the Word." Saying that she was not doing well was getting into my heart and affecting my faith for her. Speak faith by speaking the Word.

Guard the Gab

You shall not go about as a slanderer among your people,
and you are not to act against the life of your neighbor;
I am the LORD. (Leviticus 19:16)

A gossip is defined in *Merriam Webster's Collegiate Dictionary* as "a person who habitually reveals personal or sensational facts about others." There is a lack of integrity involved when someone gossips, and it causes many harmful effects. For instance, gossip can harm a friendship:

> *He who covers a transgression seeks love, but he who repeats a matter separates friends.* (Proverbs 17:9 NKJV)

We are warned by God not to gossip and not even to associate with those who do:

> *He who goes about as a slanderer reveals secrets, therefore do not associate with a gossip.* (Proverbs 20:19)

Prayer requests can actually be gossip! "We need to really pray for Mary. I'm sure she wouldn't mind my sharing this with you..." Well, maybe she would mind, so be sure to use discernment and weigh your motives very carefully before you share privileged information with anyone. Gossip can cause strife and wreak all kinds of havoc, so we must be careful not to be the one to "add fuel" to the fire:

For lack of wood the fire goes out, and where there is no whisperer, contention quiets down. Like charcoal to hot embers and wood to fire, so is a contentious man to kindle strife. (Proverbs 26:20–21)

Another very negative use of the tongue is speaking deceitful things: *"Keep your tongue from evil and your lips from speaking deceit"* (Psalm 34:13). We are also warned about speaking devious—conniving or scheming—things: *"Put away from you a deceitful mouth and put devious speech far from you"* (Proverbs 4:24).

You may think that you never do any of these things, but unless you are constantly alert to what you speak, you will fall into the trap of speaking negative words. Gossip can be very subtle, so examine your motives carefully on a daily basis.

Some years ago, we had a difficult situation arise when a staff member was speaking against my leadership. He had been corrected, but his negativity continued. I was tempted to speak back in a negative way. God showed me that returning evil for evil would never change the situation.

I began to speak goods things about the man. He did not change immediately, but at the end of six months, we experienced a miracle. This man is now my friend. The Bible says, *"When a man's ways are pleasing to the Lord, He makes even his enemies to be at peace with him"* (Proverbs 16:7)

Stop the Slander

Let all bitterness and wrath and anger and clamor and slander be put away from you, along with all malice. (Ephesians 4:31)

Therefore, putting aside all malice and all deceit and hypocrisy and envy and all slander. (1 Peter 2:1)

For the Scriptures say, "If you want to enjoy life and see many happy days, keep your tongue from speaking evil and your lips from telling lies." (1 Peter 3:10 NLT)

Loose Lips Sink Ships

There must be no filthiness and silly talk, or coarse jesting, which are not fitting, but rather giving of thanks.
(Ephesians 5:4)

Not all joking and silly talk is harmless, so set limits on how far you go in your story and joke telling. Through the years, it seems that Christians have become much more accepting of slightly off-color stories and this is partly due to changes in our culture. As Christians, we are not to be guided by our culture, which is constantly changing, but by the Word of God, which never changes.

We all love to get compliments, of course, and kind words can be very encouraging and uplifting, so speak them to others. However, watch out for flattery. The writer of Proverbs went so far as to say that a flattering mouth brings ruin:

*A lying tongue hates those it crushes, and a flattering mouth
works ruin.* (Proverbs 26:28)

*The one who guards his mouth preserves his life; the one who
opens wide his lips comes to ruin.* (Proverbs 13:3)

*Help, LORD, for the godly man ceases to be, for the
faithful disappear from among the sons of men.
They speak falsehood to one another; with flattering
lips and with a double heart they speak. May the
Lord cut off all flattering lips.* (Psalm 12:1–3)

There's a little saying, "Loose lips sink ships." It refers to a person
who talks too much. "Too much" is saying too many of the wrong
things. We are warned to guard our words carefully and not be too
hasty in speaking; controlling oneself is wise:

*When there are many words, transgression is unavoidable, but
he who restrains his lips is wise.* (Proverbs 10:19)

*Do you see a man who is hasty in his words? There is more
hope for a fool than for him.* (Proverbs 29:20)

*Words from the mouth of a wise man are gracious, while the
lips of a fool consume him; the beginning of his talking is folly,
and the end of it is wicked madness. Yet the fool multiplies
words. No man knows what will happen, and who can tell him
what will come after him?*
(Ecclesiastes 10:12–14)

Make certain that you don't allow yourself to use deceitful words. Also ask God for wisdom to understand the words of others, so that you won't be misled by lies.

The Power of Praise

"But an hour is coming, and now is, when the true worshipers shall worship the Father in spirit and truth; for such people the Father seeks to be His worshipers."
(John 4:23)

Another aspect of the subject of the tongue is praise. Our tongues were created to praise the Lord! God created man for fellowship, and from the beginning, we were created to praise and worship God. God still seeks those who will worship Him in spirit and in truth.

The book of Psalms tells us again and again to praise the Lord for His mighty works and to magnify His name: *"Let everything that has breath praise the LORD. Praise the Lord!"* (Psalm 150:6).

Psalms is really a collection of sacred songs and poems used in worship. Singing worship songs is one of the most effective ways to praise the Lord. Even though you may not have a beautiful singing voice, your praises are beautiful to His ear. What a wonderful way to use the tongue!

Enter His gates with thanksgiving and His courts with praise. Give thanks to Him, bless His name. (Psalm 100:4)

We are to enter God's presence with praise because it opens the door for God to do powerful things in our lives.

There is such power in an atmosphere of group praise that miracles can and do happen. An attitude of praise is a witness to unsaved people. In the early church, many unbelievers were born again because they saw the unity and praise among the believers:

And they, after worshiping Him, returned to Jerusalem with great joy, and were continually in the temple praising God. (Luke 24:52–53)

Day by day continuing with one mind in the temple, and breaking bread from house to house, they were taking their meals together with gladness and sincerity of heart, praising God and having favor with all the people. And the Lord was adding to their number day by day those who were being saved. (Acts 2:46–47)

There are numerous testimonies in the Bible of miracles happening during times of praise. When Paul and Silas were in prison, they sang praises; after a strong earthquake, their chains fell off, leaving them free to escape. The jailer's life would be forfeited if they escaped. He started to kill himself, but Paul assured him that no one had escaped, and presented the plan of salvation to the jailer. The jailer eagerly accepted the Lord because of the testimony and praise of two strong believers!

But about midnight Paul and Silas were praying and singing hymns of praise to God, and the prisoners were listening to them . . . and everyone's chains were unfastened . . . he [the jailer] drew his sword and was about to kill himself, supposing that the prisoners had escaped. But Paul cried out with a loud voice, saying, "Do not harm yourself, for we are all here!" ... After he [the jailer] brought them out, he said, "Sirs, what must I do to be saved?" They said, "Believe in the Lord Jesus, and you will be saved, you and your household." (Acts 16:25–31)

A Spoonful of Sugar

How sweet are your words to my taste, sweeter than honey to my mouth! (Psalm 119:103 NIV)

We are to use our tongues to build up rather than tear each other down. A word used to describe this process is "edify"—"to uplift and improve spiritually." Even when we have to say something that others may not want to hear, it can be done in love. Remember the children's song lyric, "A spoonful of sugar helps the medicine go down"? The same is true when we deal with others. Some situations may not be pleasant or easy, but loving words can help heal and encourage.

Sweet Medicine

Memorize the following verses or put them on handy note cards and use as a tonic when you need a "prescription" from the Lord.

Let no unwholesome word proceed from your mouth, but only such a word as is good for edification according to the need of the moment, so that it will give grace to those who hear. (Ephesians 4:29)

Pleasant words are a honeycomb, sweet to the soul and healing to the bones. (Proverbs 16:24)

A man has joy in an apt [unusually fit] answer, and how delightful is a timely word! (Proverbs 15:23)

Choose Wise Words

The lips of the wise spread knowledge, but the
hearts of fools are not so. (Proverbs 15:7)

To be thought of as a wise and understanding person, store up God's words of wisdom. The Word says that the righteous will utter wisdom and speak justice (see Psalm 37:30) If you are serving God with your whole heart, you *can* speak wisely.

You must make a conscious choice to exercise godly wisdom. You are wise when you keep a secret rather than revealing it:

He who goes about as a talebearer reveals secrets, but he who
is trustworthy conceals a matter. (Proverbs 11:13)

You might feel superior by telling privileged information, but the wise thing is to keep it to yourself.

Anger is a problem for many people. They speak kindly and pleasantly while things are going their way, but when something goes wrong, their tempers flare and harsh words escape their mouths. It takes discipline, but we must guard our words:

Let your speech always be with grace, seasoned, as though
seasoned with salt, so that you will know how you should
respond to each person. (Colossians 4:6)

A bridle is used on a horse to restrain and guide him. It controls and makes the animal more useful and productive. With that in mind, the Word says:

If anyone thinks himself to be religious, and yet does not bridle his tongue but deceives his own heart, this man's religion is worthless. (James 1:26)

Those are strong words; *The Amplified Bible, Classic Edition* translates the last phrase as: *"... This person's religious service is worthless (futile, barren)."* All our efforts for the Lord could be damaged if we don't watch our words: *"He who guards his mouth and his tongue, guards his soul from troubles"* (Proverbs 21:23). We have a choice!

Just Ask Dad

Be anxious for nothing, but in everything by prayer and supplication with thanksgiving let your requests be made known to God. And the peace of God, which surpasses all comprehension, will guard your hearts and your minds in Christ Jesus. (Philippians 4:6–7)

God made a way for us to be free from worry and anxiety, but too many people continue to carry their burdens. Maybe the desire to be "in control" keeps them from giving their burdens to the Lord.

Several years ago, three major things hit me at one time: my mother learned that she had a brain tumor, our son was having problems, and we were in a tremendous financial struggle in our ministry. Thank God, I instantly knew that the devil was trying to steal from us: my mother's health, my son, and finances that would pay our bills.

I began to pray! I let God know our needs and then I went to His Word. I spoke the Word to the afflicted area of my mother's brain and I spoke the Word to my son and his situation. The financial matter was the hardest struggle. While ministering at another church, the Lord led me to stand in faith for their budget, even though we were in great need ourselves.

I said "Lord, you want me to believe for their big budget when I'm going through a difficult financial trial myself?" I began to murmur and to speak negative words. I complained about having to work so hard—studying, traveling, and memorizing the Word.

In the middle of my complaining, God spoke to me out of His Word: "... *Thy God whom thou servest continually, he will deliver thee*" (Daniel 6:16 KJV). After that I had an assurance in my heart, and such a peace and confidence in Him. It was wonderful!

When the answers to prayer came, they came quickly! I got a call that my mother had gone to a brain specialist and a new x-ray showed no trace of a tumor—not even a shadow! Next, I got a call that our son had made a dramatic turnaround. After that, we had a miraculous financial breakthrough in our ministry! Your words can have a powerful effect on your life when you take your needs to God!

Speak Winning Words

First of all, then, I urge that entreaties and prayers,
petitions and thanksgivings, be made on behalf of all men,
for kings and all who are in authority, so that we may lead
a tranquil and quiet life in all godliness and dignity.
(1 Timothy 2:1–2)

Speak godly words for those in authority, for the leaders of our country, and for the leaders of other nations. God's plan includes all nations and we need to lift up the saved and our brothers and sisters in Christ in other lands. Their leaders need wisdom as much as ours do.

Just as I prayed for my mother across the miles, you can pray for the physical and spiritual needs of others.

Tame Your Tongue

> *"The tree is known by its fruit . . . For the mouth speaks out of that which fills the heart."* (Matthew 12:33–34)

Words reflect character. Some people look righteous and holy, until they open their mouths! What you say is powerful, because through your words you show the world what is in your heart:

> *For out of the abundance of the heart the mouth speaketh. A good man out of the good treasure of the heart bringeth forth good things: and an evil man out of the evil treasure bringeth forth evil things.* (Matthew 12:34–35 KJV)

Your words reveal your new nature. Believe the Word, then speak what you believe:

> *But having the same spirit of faith, according to what is written, "I BELIEVED, THEREFORE I SPOKE," we also believe, therefore we also speak.* (2 Corinthians 4:13)

Watch Your Words

"But I [Jesus] *tell you that every careless word that people speak, they shall give an accounting for it in the day of judgment. For by your words you will be justified, and by your words you will be condemned."* (Matthew 12:36–37)

You will be held accountable by God for every word you speak. Careless words can do a lot of harm, but good words can be a source of strength and creativity, bearing good fruit. Controlling your tongue can be almost impossible, but the good news is that when you put forth the effort, the Lord will help you:

For we all stumble in many ways. If anyone does not stumble in what he says, he is a perfect man, able to bridle the whole body as well. (James 3:2)

You may think, "It looks like it's hopeless, so why should I even try?" You can't completely control your tongue, but the Holy Spirit *can*! Self-control begins with your tongue.

I remember one night I was murmuring over a situation. My son Mike said, "Mother, you say, 'That what things you desire when you pray, believe that you receive them, and you shall have them.' Mother, have you really prayed about your need? If so, then don't you really believe that you will have it?"

His words were like arrows to my heart. I repented to God and my family for murmuring. We do control our attitudes and our faith with our tongue.

Full of His Word

Yielding to God means being full of His Word. Study these prayers from the Bible so they will be in your heart and help you control your tongue:

Set a guard, O LORD, over my mouth; keep watch over the door of my lips. (Psalm 141:3)

Let the words of my mouth and the meditation of my heart be acceptable in Your sight, O LORD, my rock and my Redeemer. (Psalm 19:14)

The Long Arm of the Lord

And when Jesus entered Capernaum, a centurion came to Him, imploring Him, and saying, "Lord, my servant is lying paralyzed at home, fearfully tormented." Jesus said to him, "I will come and heal him." But the centurion said, ". . . just say the word, and my servant will be healed."
(Matthew 8:5–8)

A ventriloquist trains to perfect the technique of "throwing his voice" in order to create an illusion; but we have at our disposal a supernatural gift: the ability to send the power of the Word of God into situations anywhere in the world.

A centurion came to Jesus in Capernaum and requested healing for his servant. Jesus offered to go to the centurion's home, but the centurion knew that Jesus had the power to "speak the Word" and heal his servant, no matter how far away he was. Jesus honored that faith and sent the Word that heals! (See Matthew 8:5–13.)

Another time Jesus demonstrated how the Word is sent to meet a need:

> *There was a royal official whose son was sick at Capernaum. When he heard that Jesus had come out of Judea into Galilee, he went to Him, and was imploring Him to come down and heal his son; for he was at the point of death . . . Jesus said to him, "Go; your son lives."* (John 4:46–47, 50)

When the Word of God is spoken in faith in one place, miracles can happen at another place, because God's Word is not limited by distance! You have the power to speak God's Word into situations across the country or next door. Many times, I have been separated from someone who needed prayer and I confessed the Word: *"He sent His word and healed them, and delivered them from their destructions"* (Psalm 107:20).

Use your mouth to launch the Word of God. Send it into broken homes, to sick friends, tired workers, dried-up finances, ungodly relatives . . . and watch His Word heal the situation. When sickness attacks, you can speak the Word to your own body. God wants you well: *"Beloved, I pray that in all respects you may prosper and be in good health, just as your soul prospers"* (3 John 1:2).

Target Your Problems

> *". . . if you have faith . . . you will say to this mountain, 'Move from here to there,' and it will move; and nothing will be impossible to you."* (Matthew 17:20)

Use the Word to restore a right attitude and bring reconciliation into broken relationships. Send the Word to the problem and let it be a positive force. For example, you may have hard feelings toward someone who has misused you and want to get even. Instead of speaking vengeance, express your feelings to God, confess your hatred as sin, and speak the answer: "I have the love of God in my heart and I forgive this person. By God's power, I will forget the way he/she wronged me and not try to get even." When you can "send" that Word, God will work in the situation. As you continue to confess the love of Christ for that person, you will begin to feel love:

> And hope does not disappoint, because the love of God has been poured out within our hearts through the Holy Spirit who was given to us. (Romans 5:5)

> [Love] does not act unbecomingly; it does not seek its own, is not provoked, does not take into account a wrong suffered. (1 Corinthians 13:5)

Jesus constantly declared the words He heard the Father speaking, and that is how He overcame the world: "Therefore be imitators of God, as beloved children" (Ephesians 5:1). To imitate Jesus, we must talk like our Father talks:

> "I have many things to speak and to judge concerning you, but He who sent Me is true; and the things which I heard from Him, these I speak to the world." They did not realize that He had been speaking to them about the Father. (John 8:26–27)

Action Follows the Word

"Why do you call Me, 'Lord, Lord,' and do not do what I say? Everyone who comes to Me and **hears My words and acts upon them,** *I will show you whom he is like: he is like a man building a house, who dug deep and laid a foundation upon the rock; and when a flood occurred, the torrent burst against that house an could not shake it, because it had been well built."*
(Luke 6:46–48, emphasis added)

It is vital that your actions match your words. Hear the Word, say the Word, and practice—"to do or perform often, customarily, or habitually"—the Word. If your tongue is harnessed with the power of God's Word, your deeds have to follow!

For if anyone is a hearer of the word and not a doer, he is like a man who looks at his natural face in a mirror; for once he has looked at himself and gone away, he has immediately forgotten what kind of person he was. (James 1:23–24)

You truly can change the circumstances of your life: God's Word is the key; faith is the power; and speaking the Word is the way.

STEPS TO BELIEVING BIG

1.

Read James 1:26 and James 3:1–2 in several versions of the Bible. List a few ways that you can "bridle your own tongue."

_____

_____

_____

_____

_____

_____

_____

2.

Give three or four examples of how God's Word can be used as a positive force. Use both biblical and personal examples.

_____

_____

_____

_____

_____

_____

_____

3.

Think about a negative way you may have used your
tongue. Using Scripture, write out a prayer that will
help you to avoid the same mistake in the future.

_____

_____

_____

_____

_____

_____

_____

_____

4.

Find examples of people in the Bible who spoke their
faith and received dramatic results. What habits did
they have that you can copy and apply in your own life?

_____

_____

_____

_____

_____

_____

_____

_____

5.

If we are to be imitators of God, we need to talk
like Him. Write out at least three ways you can
begin to talk like God; for instance, "God loves
the world therefore; I love those around me."

_____

_____

_____

_____

_____

_____

_____

_____

_____

_____

_____

_____

_____

_____

_____

_____

_____

_____

_____

_____

_____

4

LAUNCH YOUR FAITH

Death and life are in the power of the tongue, and those who love it will eat its fruit. (Proverbs 18:21)

As incredible as it may sound, you have the power of life and death in the words you speak. Right words can have a positive effect on every area of your life. Faith-filled words are your key to dynamic, victorious living! The instrument God created to make the Word work is your *mouth*.

Repeating and meditating on the Word of God is a powerful faith builder. Faith is not "mind over matter" or mental manipulation, but believing God's eternal, creative Word. The earth you walk on, the air you breathe, the water you drink, the sun that warms you were all *spoken* into being by God. He did it all with words. God maintains the earth with His Word . . . He keeps you with the same Word.

"Speak the word only, and my servant shall be healed."
(Matthew 8:8 KJV)

We often make faith sound too difficult. This scripture tells us that speaking the Word "only" is great faith. In the past, the Lord dealt with me about my conversation. He said, "You are not speaking the Word only, you are also speaking your doubt, unbelief, and problems."

Our words should not damage another's character, but build them up. Claim for them a positive quality in place of a negative one. Instead of being angry over someone's stubborn disposition, thank God they are steadfast in their faith.

Claim for yourself all that you know you have in Christ. Ask God for wisdom and to show you why you are angry. Perhaps He will reveal a weakness in your own character that He is eager to mend and strengthen. Acknowledge and confess your anger as sin.

Ignite Your Faith

This Book of the Law shall not depart out of your mouth, but you shall meditate on it day and night, that you may observe and do according to all that is written in it.
(Joshua 1:8 AMPC)

The Bible is full of instances where the spoken Word was used to activate faith. Joshua had been Moses's right-hand man for many years; he knew that one day Moses would die, leaving him to lead the children of Israel into the promised land. When Moses died and God told Joshua that he was in charge, things looked bleak;

Joshua no longer had someone upon whom to lean. He was on his own, so he had to take the Word of God in his mouth and put it into practice.

Joshua became successful in every area of his life because he believed what God said in His Word. Joshua flourished in his spiritual life, his family life, his finances, and his life as a leader because he disciplined himself to meditate on the Word. Only the first five books of the Bible had been written, but Joshua was faithful with what he had! Can you imagine meditating on and speaking the books of Leviticus and Numbers day and night?

Joshua was over 80 years old when he took charge of the Israelites. Yet many of us feel like we're "over the hill" at 50, blaming our age for loss of memory and energy. Joshua proved that it doesn't have to be that way. He was exceptionally busy leading a nation of over a million people. He was not only their spiritual and military leader, but responsible for providing their clothes, water, and food.

Speaking and meditating on God's Word gave Joshua incredible military success. The walls of Jericho fell because he directed the people to march around them for six days and to shout on the seventh. They shouted in obedience to the instructions God had given: "*Joshua said to the people, 'Shout, for the LORD has given you the city'*" (Joshua 6:16 NKJV). You can do the same—shout your troubles away.

During another battle, God sent huge hailstones that battered the enemy, but missed Joshua and his men:

As they fled before Israel, while they were descending [the pass] to Beth-horon, the Lord cast great stones from the

heavens on them as far as Azekah, killing them. More died
because of the hailstones than the Israelites slew with the
sword. (Joshua 10:11 AMPC)

Can you imagine the hand of a Canaanite on your throat when
suddenly he is knocked to the ground by a huge hailstone? Our
miracle-working God commands natural events and protects His
children. We can be just as victorious in our lives as the Israelites.

You Can Have a Double Portion, Too

When they had finished dividing the land for inheritance by
their boundaries, the Israelites gave an inheritance among
them to Joshua son of Nun. According to the word of the Lord
they gave him the city for which he asked—Timnath-serah
in the hills of Ephraim. And he built the city and dwelt in it.
(Joshua 19:49–50 AMPC)

Joshua was a great warrior, but was he prosperous in other areas
of his life? Yes, he was successful in business. When the promised
land was taken, he became very wealthy when he received a large
mountainous tract of land. It was named *Timnath-serah*, which
means "double portion—city of the sun." God saw to it that Joshua
got what he wanted in life.

What about Joshua's family and home life? Was he successful
there? Yes, Joshua was very successful at home. The Word had
worked for him as a military commander and businessman, but
home is where it really counts. At the end of Joshua's life, he summed
up his success by challenging others to live as he had lived:

... Choose for yourselves this day whom you will serve ... but as for me and my house, we will serve the Lord.
(Joshua 24:15 AMPC)

Joshua made the choice to speak God's Word, and the result was great success. If it worked for Joshua, it will work for you! You have God's Word just like Joshua. Start speaking the Word into every situation and watch your life change: *"But the word is very nigh unto thee, in thy mouth..."* (Deuteronomy 30:14 KJV). You activate faith with your mouth by saying what God says. Try it! You'll never be the same!

Shout Down Your Giants

... "We should by all means go up and take possession of it, for we shall surely overcome it." But the men who had gone up with him said, "... we became like grasshoppers in our own sight, so we were in their sight." (Numbers 13:30–33)

Are you facing a giant in your life today—a physical ailment, marital problem, lack of finances, difficulty with your children, or strife at work? Any situation can seem overwhelming.

> **You are in covenant relationship with the God who created the universe.**

Compared to your problems, you may feel small as a grasshopper, but your feelings are wrong. You are in covenant relationship with the God who created the universe. God will fight on your side no matter how big or small you feel. Like David against Goliath, you can fight your giants with confidence, armed with the Word of God. Don't be deceived into believing that you can't win when problems seem so much bigger than you. Practice your covenant relationship with God and shout His promises at your mountains!

You Are Not A Grasshopper... You Are A Victor!

All these blessings shall come upon you and overtake you, if you will obey the LORD your God... The LORD will cause your enemies who rise up against you to be defeated before you; they will come out against you one way and will flee before you seven ways... The LORD shall make you the head and not the tail, and you only will be above, and you will not be underneath, if you listen to the commandments of the LORD your God, which I charge you today, to observe them carefully. (Deuteronomy 28:2, 7, 13)

The Word Is Your Circle of Power

The word of the Lord spread widely and grew in power.
(Acts 19:20 NIV)

The Philistines were enemies of Israel and their champion warrior, Goliath, was literally a giant. They had gathered their armies to battle at a place called Socoh, which means "hedge, enclosure, or shut-in place." Socoh was located in *Judah*, which means "praise."

When you praise the Lord, a hedge is built around you, shutting you in with God. Think of being shut in with God! You may not feel like rejoicing because of the trial, but you can rejoice because of the victory you will receive! *"Consider it all joy, my brethren, when you encounter various trials"* (James 1:2). Where does this "joy" come from? It comes from those times of being shut in with Him.

> *The joy of the Lord is your strength and stronghold.*
> (Nehemiah 8:10 AMPC)

Junior Giant Killer

> *And Saul said to David, thou art not able to go against this*
> *Philistine to fight with him; for thou art but a youth.*
> (1 Samuel 17:33 KJV)

The Philistines and the Israelites were gathered on opposite mountaintops, with a large valley between them. Goliath boasted to Israel that if anyone could kill him, the Philistines would be their servants. Your giant can become your servant. This realization is vital! Let God's Word be your weapon and allow the problems in your life to take you to a higher place in God.

Goliath wasn't defeated at once, however. For 40 days he shouted at the Israelites, taunting and ridiculing them, causing them to fear for their lives. Goliath challenged them to find a man who would fight him, but Saul and all his men were fearful:

> *And the Philistine said, I defy the ranks of Israel this day; give*
> *me a man, that we may fight together. When Saul and all*
> *Israel heard those words of the Philistine, they were dismayed*
> *and greatly afraid.* (1 Samuel 17:10–11 AMPC)

This is a tactic your enemy uses: he wants you to be overwhelmed by the problem, instead of the other way around. The Philistines shouted about how mighty they were and convinced the Israelites that they were weak and useless. That's exactly what the devil wants you to think, too, but you have an example in David. He was not impressed with the enemy and he was not afraid of the giant—David was impressed with the power of the God of Israel and was ready to do battle in God's strength.

Just as Goliath shouted out threats to David of what "might happen," the devil attacks our minds with thoughts of bad things that can happen to us. David wasn't a soldier; he was just a boy who took food to his brothers serving in the army. When he heard the giant bellow his challenge, he was astonished that someone would have the nerve to defy the armies of God:

Who is this uncircumcised Philistine that he should defy the armies of the living God? (1 Samuel 17:26 AMPC)

David took one look at the situation and saw the battle for what it was: the devil's army against God's army rather than the Philistines against the Israelites. David was so amazed that Saul's army was afraid and not proclaiming victory, he volunteered to go against the enemy himself.

The devil will use people to try to discourage you. David, however, did a very important thing: he told Saul about his many victories against lions and bears, and made a strong statement of faith.

David said, The Lord Who delivered me out of the paw of the lion and out of the paw of the bear, He will deliver me out of the hand of this Philistine. (1 Samuel 17:37 AMPC)

When problems come your way, remember what the Lord has done for you in the past—rehearse your victories—then speak your faith.

King Saul told David to go ahead and fight Goliath, blessed him, and tried to give him his armor, but it was too big. David knew what would protect him and it was godly armor—the Word of the Lord! When Goliath lumbered toward David screaming insults, David calmly replied:

You come to me with a sword, a spear, and a javelin, but I come to you in the name of the Lord of hosts, the God of the ranks of Israel, whom you have defied.
(1 Samuel 17:45 AMPC)

That was David's way of saying, "You aren't defying me, you're defying the Lord God, and you had better watch out!" David knew the power of Israel's covenant with God.

Five Smooth Stones

Then he took his staff in his hand, chose five smooth stones from the stream, put them in the pouch of his shepherd's bag and, with his sling in his hand, approached the Philistine. (1 Samuel 17:40 NIV)

Just as David collected five smooth stones for ammunition, you need to have more than one scripture in your arsenal. David wasn't afraid that he would miss Goliath with the first stone, he just wanted to be prepared for the unexpected. Satan may try to toss unexpected things at you, adding to your problems, so you need "stones" of the Word to hurl at him to win the victory.

Goliath was not an ordinary, run-of-the-mill enemy. He was enormous and wore massive armor. A heavy bronze helmet covered his head, so how could David kill him? This was a great part of the miracle. The one stone David threw must have penetrated the helmet covering the giant's forehead, although ordinarily a stone would bounce off metal. David's confession of faith made that stone pierce through the bronze, the flesh, and the bone. The stone sank into the giant's forehead and he fell over. David didn't have a sword, so he ran to the giant, and using his own sword, cut off his head! Remember, it's not good enough to knock out a problem—you must cut off the problem at its source so it will not return to attack you again!

How astonished the Philistines were when they saw their champion defeated! Chased by the Israelites, they ran in despair to a place called Ekron, which means "eradication." When we throw the Word like a stone, we eradicate—"get rid of and wipe out"—the enemy. What David did next shows that he was a very wise young man. Instead of basking in the glory of his victory, he took Goliath's head back to Jerusalem, the city of peace, where God was worshiped. He wanted to be sure that God received all the glory and praise for this great victory.

Shh! Your Body's Listening

"What I always feared has happened to me.
What I dreaded has come true." (Job 3:25 NLT)

Medical research shows that the actions of the body are related to the tongue. A neurosurgeon said that the speech nerve center has power over the entire body. Speaking can give you control over your body to manipulate it in the way you wish. He said that if someone continually says, "I'm going to become weak," then the nerves receive that message, and say, "Let's prepare to become weak. We've received instructions that we should become weak." They then adjust their physical attitudes to weakness. If you say, "I have no ability to do this job," right away your body begins to declare the same thing.

It is no wonder Jesus emphasized the importance of our words! When we realize the impact our words have on the natural nervous system, we can begin to understand their impact in the spiritual realm. Truly, what you say and believe will happen:

> *Truly I tell you, whoever says to this mountain, Be lifted up*
> *and thrown into the sea! and does not doubt at all in his heart*
> *but believes that what he says will take place, it will be done*
> *for him.* (Mark 11:23 AMPC)

It is so important to say what is true and right, the things that God says in His Word. Instead of saying, "I know I'm going to be achy and weak tomorrow because I've caught the flu," say, "I am strong because God is my refuge and strength" (see Psalm 46:1).

Rather than saying, "I'm a failure; I just can't do it!" say, *"I can do all things through Christ who strengthens me"* (Philippians 4:13 NKJV).

Winning the God Way

> *And when the tempter came to him, he said, If thou be the Son of God, command that these stones be made bread. But he [Jesus] answered and said, It is written, Man shall not live by bread alone, but by every word that proceedeth out of the mouth of God... And [Satan] saith unto him [Jesus], If thou be the Son of God, cast thyself down: for it is written, He shall give his angels charge concerning thee: and in their hands they shall bear thee up, lest at any time thou dash thy foot against a stone. Jesus said unto him, It is written again, Thou shalt not tempt the Lord thy God.* (Matthew 4:3–4, 6–7 KJV)

Jesus used the Word many times during His ministry on earth, but especially when He was tempted by Satan. The devil even tried to trick Jesus by quoting Scripture. Beware! Satan is a tricky, devious enemy and he will use every tactic to defeat you. Every time the devil tempted Jesus, He was ready with a quick answer: "It is written!"

You might think that would settle the matter, but the devil is persistent; he didn't give up. He tried a third time to entice Jesus to sin, on this occasion with possessions and worldly goods: *"All these things will I give thee, if thou wilt fall down and worship me"* (Matthew 4:9 KJV). This is a difficult temptation for people today.

Jesus grew weary of Satan's games and took a strong stand against him: *"Then Jesus said to him, Begone, Satan! For it has been written, You shall worship the Lord your God, and Him alone shall you serve"* (Matthew 4:10 AMPC). In times of temptation, you should do exactly the same thing. Use the Word and you will escape. God will honor His Word and show you a way out, a pathway to success:

No temptation has overtaken you but such as is common to man; and God is faithful, who will not allow you to be tempted beyond what you are able, but with the temptation will provide the way of escape also, that you may be able to endure it. (1 Corinthians 10:13)

Say to Satan, *"It is written!"* Use the power of the Word. Jesus shows us clearly how to fight in times of temptation. When He commanded Satan to leave, *"Then the devil departed from Him, and behold, angels came and ministered to Him"* (Matthew 4:11 AMPC). What a comforting thought!

Speaking the Word works! Many years ago, a man in our church was in an accident, and his finger was cut off. He was put into a pressure chamber, which caused him to have a stroke and a heart attack. He was 42 years old; the doctors said he wouldn't live 24 hours. If he did live, he would be a vegetable.

My late husband, Wally, and I spoke the Word over him. We stood on the Scriptures and believed he was going to live, not die or become a vegetable. We, along with our youth pastor, went to the hospital every day and spoke the Word concerning healing over him. Not long after we prayed, that man walked the aisles of our church. He's a living, breathing, walking miracle and testimony that the Word works—if you work it.

Confession Defined

Nelson's Illustrated Bible Dictionary defines confession as "an admission of sins and the profession of belief in the doctrines of a particular faith."

"We maintain our faith by keeping our confession in line with the Word of God. Since faith is released by our mouth, the importance of speaking the right words—making the right confession—cannot be overstated."

"Since God cannot lie, we cannot lie when our confession is what God says. For example, we are who God says we are, we have what God says we have, and we can do what God says we can do. We should be confessing who we are, what we have, and what we can do by faith, regardless of whether we can see it or feel it. Our confession is our belief of who we are in Christ Jesus."

Pray Your Faith

Pray, therefore like this: Our Father Who is in heaven, hallowed (kept holy) be Your name. Your kingdom come, Your will be done on earth as it is in heaven. Give us this day our daily bread. And forgive us our debts, as we also have forgiven (left, remitted, and let go of the debts, and given up resentment against) our debtors. And lead (bring) us not into temptation, but deliver us from the evil one. For Yours is the kingdom and the power and the glory forever. Amen. (Matthew 6:9–13 AMPC)

You can pray more powerful and faith-filled prayers. You can be delivered from evil and learn to forgive by praying according to the will of the Father, and by speaking His Word into your situation. When you pray the Word specifically for your need, you will receive powerful answers. You are probably familiar with the Lord's Prayer, but do you realize it can be an expression of faith for a supernatural blessing?

Praying the words *"Thy will be done"* is not a cop-out phrase or an excuse for not taking charge of things. When you pray for God's will, and really mean it, you're going to get God's very best. Your faith is turned loose! You can be assured that He will hear you:

> *This is the confidence which we have before Him, that, if we ask anything according to His will, He hears us. And if we know that He hears us in whatever we ask, we know that we have the requests which we have asked from Him.*
> (1 John 5:14–15)

The Lord's Prayer can be divided into six parts: three petitions have to do with God and His glory, and three have to do with our own needs. It is the perfect Bible lesson on speaking your faith. When you pray *"Our Father,"* you not only petition the God of the universe, but your personal Father God. There is awesome power in the name "Father," but there is also a close loving relationship because we are God's family—His sons and daughters. He loves us dearly!

The kingdom of God transcends time, which means it isn't limited by seasons. God is able and willing to do the same miraculous things today as He has done in the past. When we pray for

God to *"give us our daily bread,"* we show the Lord that we trust Him to meet our present personal needs.

"Forgive us our debts as we forgive our debtors" indicates that our Father is able to forgive our sins and help us forgive those who have wronged us. *"Lead us not into temptation but deliver us from the evil one"* provides our protection from the schemes of Satan to steal from, kill, or destroy us. Temptation, as used here, means "testing," which comes from the devil. Although "tests" can be unpleasant, they can be the keys to our success in life. God has already made provision for all your needs, so your confession of faith is based on the truth of the Word.

The Prayers of Paul

Paul used prayer to bless others and bring good into their lives. In his love for Jesus and the church, Paul prayed ardently to God, asking Him to be generous to them:

[For I always pray to] the God of our Lord Jesus Christ, the Father of glory, that He may grant you a spirit of wisdom and revelation [of insight into mysteries and secrets] in the [deep and intimate] knowledge of Him.
(Ephesians 1:17 AMPC)

For this reason we also, from the day we heard of it, have not ceased to pray and make [special] request for you, [asking] that you may be filled with the full (deep and clear) knowledge of His will in all spiritual wisdom [in comprehensive insight into the ways and purposes of God] and in understanding and discernment of spiritual things.
(Colossians 1:9 AMPC)

Open the Floodgates of Faith

So will My word be which goes forth from My mouth;
it shall not return to Me empty, without accomplishing
what I desire, and without succeeding in the matter
for which I sent it. (Isaiah 55:11)

Your ability to release your faith depends upon your ability to allow the life of Jesus to flow through you. He is the vine, we are the branches. He gives life to the branches and is their total support system:

"Abide in Me, and I in you. As the branch cannot bear fruit
of itself, unless it abides in the vine, so neither can you, unless
you abide in Me." (John 15:4)

"Abiding in Him" means that you have sustained continual communion with Him through prayer and His Word (see John 15:7). If God's Word constantly abides in you, you will be instantly ready to confess it: *"Out of the abundance (overflow) of the heart his mouth speaks"* (Luke 6:45 AMPC).

God's Word shows you how to ask Him wisely for the things you need. As you ask in God's will, guided by the Holy Spirit, and using the Word, He will grant your request. As you *"abide"* in Him, the Holy Spirit will prompt you to ask for the right things. God's Word will teach you how to have continual communion with Him.

STEPS TO BELIEVING BIG

1.

Keep a journal of the times God has proven Himself faithful to you. Rehearse your victories and have them available for the enemy's next attack.

_____

_____

_____

_____

_____

_____

_____

2.

Look for opportunities to speak God's Word to bless others. List three things you are believing for and put a Bible verse with each one that demonstrates "confessing" the Word. Speak your confessions daily until you have the answers.

_____

_____

_____

_____

_____

_____

_____

3.

Read the Lord's Prayer in several different versions of the Bible. Meditate on how God meets your needs. Study John 15:1–16 and write out a personal plan for "abiding" in Him.

_____
_____
_____
_____
_____
_____
_____
_____
_____
_____
_____
_____
_____
_____
_____
_____
_____
_____
_____
_____
_____
_____
_____
_____
_____
_____
_____

5

FEAR: FAITH'S MORTAL ENEMY

For God hath not given us the spirit of fear; but of power, and of love, and of a sound mind. (2 Timothy 1:7 KJV)

Just as we use the word faith to express believing for something good, we use the word fear to express believing in something bad. That is why fear makes faith fruitless, but faith can cancel out fear. Fear is your foe. God does not want you to live in fear, and He has equipped you to deal with it. You have the wisdom to discern your enemy and the weapon to fight him, and win!

Both faith and fear can motivate you and cause you to act. God's Word will empower you to function in faith, so you will step out and act in the way God instructs. On the other hand, fear will cause you to move in the opposite direction. You will avoid the battle, run away, and be chased by the devil when in fact, you are supposed to chase him! *"Submit therefore to God. Resist the devil and he will flee from you"* (James 4:7).

There is a clear relationship between fear and faith: both originate from the information you receive. Faith is built on information from God and His Word. Fear is based on negative information from the devil through neighbors, doctors, newspapers, weather reports, and news reports. Fear is believing the bad news. Fear is actually faith in something you don't want to happen.

Know Your Enemy

The word "fear" comes from the root word *phobos*, meaning: "to be intimidated by the enemy, to be in dread or terror." A phobia is considered an irrational fear; a fear that is based on an unrealistic expectation of something that might happen. What terrifies you? What intimidates you? What do you dread?

Perhaps your fears are not easily identified. Simple insecurity, a lack of confidence in yourself, can be a byproduct of fear: "What if I try, but fail? What will people think of me? I'm afraid I'm not good enough." Many times, I have awakened in the night and started to worry. Then I'd catch myself and bring to mind Proverbs 16:3, *"Commit your works to the LORD and your plans will be established."* The devil would like to harass us through our thought-life. However, if we will commit our works to the Lord, our thought-life will come into line.

We have all had negative thoughts at one time or another, but you can learn to take control of such thoughts. God has given you a *"sound mind!"* Put faith in the place of fear and the fear will disappear. You can become *aphobos*—"without fear." Pray Luke 1:74, *"To grant us that we, being rescued from the hand of our enemies, might serve Him without fear."*

A better understanding of what fear actually is will help you war against it. There are other root words for fear, such as: *deilia*, which means "cowardice and timidity." Several Bible versions of 2 Timothy 1:7 translate fear as "timidity," but God has given us the power to overcome the fears that attack us.

Likewise, the root word *pachad*—"to be on guard, having a fear of death"—is directly neutralized in the Word. God will *"...free those who through fear of death were subject to slavery all their lives"* (Hebrews 2:15).

It is Satan's desire to keep you bound by fear all your life because if fear is your ruler, you can't act in faith. You will be an exile in enemy territory, afraid to claim your inheritance, use supernatural weapons, or declare whom you serve. Remember, God in you overcomes the enemy:

> *You are from God, little children, and have overcome them; because greater is He who is in you than he who is in the world.* (1 John 4:4)

Good Fear

> *Let all the earth fear the LORD; let all the inhabitants of the world stand in awe of Him. For He spoke, and it was done; He commanded, and it stood fast.* (Psalm 33:8–9)

Another type of fear worth mentioning is *eulabeia*, translated as "caution and reverence; godly, holy, and reverent fear." This is not a *negative* fear. There is a beautiful worship song that includes the phrase, "Mighty God, to whom all praise is due, I stand in awe of You." It means that we look upon our Lord and Savior with wonder and reverence. This is godly, holy fear; and if we are to have a right relationship with our loving Father, we will have this type of "fear" of Him. You can choose the God-given, healthy fear, *eulabeia*.

Walking on Water

And He said, "Come!" And Peter got out of the boat, and walked on the water and came toward Jesus. But seeing the wind, he became frightened, and beginning to sink, he cried out, "Lord, save me!" (Matthew 14:29–30)

Peter was doing fine walking on the water until he looked around and focused on his circumstances. As soon as he took his eyes off Jesus, doubt overtook him, and fear overcame him.

His senses took over: his ears heard the howling of the wind; even though it was dark, his eyes may have seen the storm clouds moving; his body felt the thrust of the waves; an awareness of danger gave way to anxiety and fear, and he took his eyes off the goal—Jesus! Even though Jesus was close by, Peter let fear come in, and because he did so, he began to sink. Jesus's response to this fear-filled disciple was to rescue him by reaching out and holding him up. He also rebuked him: *"You of little faith, why did you doubt?"* (Matthew 14:31).

Both faith and fear will grow a crop in your life. Faith will yield a harvest of God's best; fear will yield the devil's worst: *"For what I fear comes upon me, and what I dread befalls me"* (Job 3:25). God constantly warns us, "Do not fear!" Fear will produce the very thing we don't want.

"Do Not Fear!"

Have not I commanded thee? Be strong and of a good courage;
be not afraid, neither be thou dismayed: for the LORD thy God
is with thee whithersoever thou goest. (Joshua 1:9 KJV)

When our son Michael was 16 or 17, he wanted to buy a car. He found one and the seller, a pastor, let him bring it home to try it out. Early the next morning I went to wake him, but he wasn't in his room. When I saw His window open, I felt very uneasy.

Running to the front of the house, I looked out the window and the car was missing. My heart instantly filled with fear. I thought, "Oh, dear God, where is my son?" I was almost overcome with fear, and wild thoughts started running through my mind.

> **Fear will produce the very thing we don't want.**

I thought, "Lord, he's got that pastor's car, and he doesn't even have a driver's license. If he gets caught driving—it could really be serious."

You know what it's like to be fearful—your heart begins to pound, and your breath gets shallow. Finally, I turned to the Lord, "God, I don't want to be overwhelmed by fear—fill me with faith! Please, quickly give me a scripture." The Lord reminded me of Haggai 2:5:

*"As for the promise which I made you when you came out
of Egypt, My Spirit is abiding in your midst; do not fear!"*

I could almost hear the Lord saying, "Marilyn, I brought you
out of the world and I have a covenant with you. You belong to
me, so don't be afraid. My Spirit is with you and I'll take care of
this." All day we wondered where Michael was, and all day I quoted
that scripture to keep my fear at bay.

Michael was to be at work at 5 o'clock that afternoon, and when
we called his place of employment, he was there! He and the car
were both safe. Because I had fought fear with the Word, I had
peace even before we knew that Michael was all right.

The Garden of Fear

Many fears are picked up in childhood and carried throughout life.
The fears of parents can be transferred to children through words
and actions. Even offhand remarks by an adult can impact a child
forever. Generational curses of fear, if not broken, can immobilize
you later in life.

Whatever the source of your fear, however, ultimately it is a
tool of the devil to keep you in bondage and drive out your faith
in God. Satan uses bad news, well-meaning friends, and adverse
circumstances to cause you to doubt and fear. If you dwell on
negative things, the enemy will prevent you from taking your
"promised land":

*But the men who had gone up with him [Caleb] said, "We are
not able to go up against the people, for they are too strong*

for us." So they gave out to the sons of Israel a bad report of the land which they had spied out, saying, "The land through which we have gone, in spying it out, is a land that devours its inhabitants; and all the people whom we saw in it are men of great size . . . and we became like grasshoppers in our own sight, and so we were in their sight." (Numbers 13:31–33)

The 12 spies that Moses sent to explore the land saw beautiful and wonderful things, but they also saw giants and heavily fortified cities. Ten of the spies emphasized the negative, but two, Joshua and Caleb, said with great confidence, "We can overcome and conquer!" (See Numbers 14:5–10.) They all had heard God's promise concerning the land of Canaan, but ten of the twelve let their fears blind their faith. They let Satan destroy their self-image. Compared to the giants, they saw themselves as little *"grasshoppers."* They became losers instead of winners in their own eyes.

If you give in to it, fear will become your master and hold you in slavery to things from which God wants to set you free. Fear that they won't receive healing keeps some people sick. On the other hand, in a twisted way, some people don't really want to be healed. They fear they will not be able to handle new responsibilities. Fear is certainly a crippling, cruel taskmaster!

Don't Worry—Be Happy!

Casting the whole of your care [all your anxieties, all your worries, all your concerns, once and for all] on Him, for He cares for you affectionately and cares about you watchfully.
(1 Peter 5:7 AMPC)

Worry is another byproduct of fear. A fearful person is worried, anxious, and constantly wondering what terrible event will happen next. It is extremely hard to trust God when you are worrying, because anxiety is a hindrance to your faith. Being "happy" isn't denying fear but getting rid of your worries by giving them to Jesus. Trust the Lord and begin to thank Him for the answer even as you make your requests known to Him:

Be anxious for nothing, but in everything by prayer and supplication with thanksgiving let your requests be made known to God. (Philippians 4:6)

Fear and unbelief head the list of sins that lead to eternal death. Those who are afraid to trust Jesus in this life will have to be without Him for eternity:

But the fearful, and unbelieving, and the abominable, and murderers, and whore mongers, and sorcerers, and idolaters, and all liars, shall have their part in the lake which burneth with fire and brimstone. (Revelation 21:8 KJV)

Fear of Sin

And they brought to Him a paralytic lying on a bed. Seeing their faith, Jesus said to the paralytic, "Take courage, son; your sins are forgiven."... "Which is easier, to say, 'Your sins are forgiven,' or to say, 'Get up, and

walk'?"... then He said to the paralytic, "Get up, pick up
your bed, and go home." (Matthew 9:2, 5–6)

The paralyzed man brought to Jesus by his friends was sick and fearful, afraid of the consequences of his sin. Jesus stepped right into the situation and told the man to have courage—because his sins were forgiven! Then, he could be healed.

If the fear of sin is causing you or your loved ones to be sick, take courage. Jesus is interceding for you right now:

For there is one God, and one mediator also between
God and men, the man Christ Jesus. (1 Timothy 2:5)

Hope Overcomes Fear

And a woman who had been suffering from a hemorrhage
for twelve years, came up behind Him and touched the fringe
of His cloak; for she was saying to herself, "If I only touch His
garment, I will get well." But Jesus turning and seeing her said,
"Daughter, take courage; your faith has made you well." At
once the woman was made well. (Matthew 9:20–22)

In the time of Christ, a woman with a hemorrhage (issue of blood) was not allowed to mingle with the public, because she was considered "unclean." Such women weren't even allowed to go to the temple. They were not respected and largely ignored.

Therefore, the woman who was healed when she touched the hem of Jesus's robe had to be rather sneaky in her approach to Him. She was convinced that if she could just get to where He was, she would be healed! Her hope for a cure overcame her fear of being caught and punished.

Once again Jesus told someone to *"take courage."* This woman had to overcome her fear and move in faith. She released the power of the Word by acting out her faith for healing, and was rewarded when Jesus told her, *"Your faith has made you well."*

Illness can produce fear, just as fear can produce illness. So, it is essential that you stay in control and focused on God's promises, otherwise your mind will become Satan's playground. He will try to torment you with irrational and unfounded thoughts. You need not fear, however, because Jesus is aware of your helplessness, and He has already dealt with every physical ailment:

> *He sent His word and healed them, and delivered them from their destructions.* (Psalm 107:20)

Call on Him

Even when we are walking in the perfect will of God, fearful circumstances occur because this earth is still in the possession of the enemy. Natural conditions such as blizzards, tornadoes, or earthquakes can give you a feeling of total helplessness but knowing you can call on God to save you is a great comfort.

Even though Peter and the other disciples were battling a storm, rowing in the dark, and scared half to death, they were right where Jesus had sent them. They did not know it, but Jesus had not left them alone. He had followed along to help them. Jesus recognized their fear and immediately calmed them with these words: *"Take courage, it is I; do not be afraid"* (Matthew 14:27).

God's Pattern for Healing

- Act on your faith and not on your fear (2 Timothy 1:7).

- Repent of your sins, including your fears, to God (Luke 13: 3, 5).

- Tell your mountain (illness) to depart (Mark 11:22–23).

- Have the elders of the church anoint you with oil (James 5:14–15).

- Pray the prayer of faith (John 15:7).

- Speak the Word of life over your body daily (Proverbs 4:20–22).

Paranoia or Power?

For our struggle is not against flesh and blood, but against the rulers, against the powers, against the world forces of this darkness, against the spiritual forces of wickedness in the heavenly places. Therefore, take up the full armor of God, that you may be able to resist in the evil day. (Ephesians 6:12–13)

Have you ever felt like you were in danger? We all try to use common sense to avoid dark alleys or unsafe situations, but physical danger is not the only thing that can threaten us. Your co-workers could say things about you behind your back. You might feel threatened by people at church. Your fears may even be well-founded. Rather than trying to fight and defend yourself in the natural, learn to turn the conflict over to God:

The fear of man brings a snare, but he who trusts in the LORD *will be exalted.* (Proverbs 29:25)

His Peace

When Jesus speaks, peace prevails, no matter what is going on in your life: *"Peace I leave with you; My peace I give to you; not as the world gives do I give to you. Do not let your heart be troubled, nor let it be fearful"* (John 14:27).

When the Apostle Paul stood to speak before the Sanhedrin in Jerusalem, he could have been afraid:

And as a great dissension was developing, the commander was afraid Paul would be torn to pieces by them . . . But on the night immediately following, the Lord stood at his side and said, "Take courage; for as you have solemnly witnessed to My cause at Jerusalem, so you must witness at Rome also." (Acts 23:10–11)

Paul's life was in danger, but he didn't run away. He was bold! He knew he was supposed to take the gospel to Rome, and nothing could stop him or his godly assignment. You, too, can be bold in God:

When I am afraid, I will put my trust in You. In God, whose word I praise, In God I have put my trust; I shall not be afraid. What can mere man do to me? (Psalm 56:3–4)

As Jesus spent time with His disciples, they began to realize that He would not always be with them and that it wasn't popular or safe to be His follower. Persecution was not appealing; in fact, it was a frightening possibility. Jesus reassured them:

These things I have spoken to you, so that in Me you may have peace. In the world you have tribulation, but take courage; I have overcome the world. (John 16:33)

Fearless, Faithless, or Foolish?

"Simon, Simon, behold, Satan has demanded permission to sift you like wheat; but I have prayed for you, that your faith may not fail; and you, when once you have turned again, strengthen your brothers." (Luke 22:31–32)

Jesus prayed that Simon Peter's faith would not fail—and it didn't! "Well, it sure sounds like it failed—several times," you might say. No, it wasn't *his faith* that failed, it was his courage. Peter loved Jesus with all his heart and Jesus knew that, and He understood Peter's struggle with fear just as He understands yours.

Peter knew who Jesus was: *"You are the Christ, the Son of the living God"* (Matthew 16:16 AMPC). But when Jesus told the disciples that He must go to Jerusalem and be killed, Peter, speaking emotionally, rebuked Jesus: *"God forbid it, Lord! This shall never happen to You"* (Matthew 16:22). Peter denied Jesus's purpose on earth because he feared losing Jesus. We, too, can speak emotionally and in the flesh, to deny what God would and could do for us.

Why was Peter so emotional and afraid? He didn't understand

that the cross was to be a supernatural place of victory, not defeat! He didn't know that *Jesus had to go to the cross!*

After the crucifixion, Peter was depressed and discouraged. He decided to go fishing and convinced several of the disciples to go with him. They fished all night and caught nothing. When morning came, they saw a man on the shore who said, "Children, you haven't caught any fish, have you?" and He told them exactly where to cast the net (see John 21). When their nets were instantly full of fish, John recognized the Messiah and told the others:

> . . . *It is the Lord! Simon Peter, hearing him* [John] *say that it was the Lord, put (girded) on his upper garment (his fisherman's coat, his outer tunic) for he was stripped [for work]—and sprang into the sea.* (John 21:7 AMPC)

Jesus had built a fire on the shore and invited the men to bring their fish and eat with him. After breakfast, He spoke to Peter. He wanted to be sure Peter heard him, so He called him Simon, "the listening one":

> *Simon, son of John, do you love Me more that these [others do—with reasoning, intentional, spiritual devotion, as one loves the Father]?* (John 21:15 AMPC)

Three times Jesus asked Peter if he loved Him, and three times Peter replied that he did. What was the significance of this? Three times Peter had denied Jesus and now three times he declared his deep love for Him.

In his loving way, Jesus let Peter know that when his time to die came, he would be able to resist fear. History records that Peter was crucified for his faith, but he insisted on being hung upside down. He felt unworthy to die in the same manner as his Lord. Peter truly triumphed over his fear! The cross sets you free to live your new life unhindered by the fears of the old life, filled with power from on high! The love of the Lord can set you free from fear:

> God is love, and he who abides in love abides in God, and God in him. Love has been perfected among us in this: that we may have **boldness** in the day of judgment; because as He is, so are we in this world. There is **no fear** in love; but perfect love casts out fear, because fear involves torment. But he who fears has not been made perfect in love.
> (1 John 4:16–18 NKJV, emphasis added)

Unconquered by Fear

Despite the fact that he was a servant, Daniel let the Word of God make him the conqueror. Nebuchadnezzar, king of Babylon, had overcome Jerusalem. Daniel, and three of his friends, being of the royal tribe of Judah, were among the first captured. The Bible records how handsome, smart, and accomplished they were. Daniel was a young man of excellent character, wise beyond his years, and poised enough to stand before kings:

> Youths without blemish, well-favored in appearance and skillful in all wisdom, discernment, and understanding, apt in learning knowledge, competent to stand and serve in the king's palace. (Daniel 1:4 AMPC)

The king changed their names to try to change their identities: they became known as Shadrach, Meshach, and Abednego—and Belteshazzar. Daniel, however, refused to change his image and his identity to serve a foreign god. The world will try to get you to change your image of yourself, but you must continue to see yourself as God sees you.

"*But Daniel made up his mind not to eat the food and wine given to them by the king*" (Daniel 1:8 TLB). Daniel requested a healthy diet that he knew would build his strength and endurance. He asked the chief servant to give him and his companions only vegetables and water for ten days, then compare them with the others at the end of that time:

> *Now God granted Daniel favor and compassion in the sight of the commander of the officials.* (Daniel 1:9)

You know, of course, that Daniel and his companions fared well in this comparison:

> *And at the end of ten days it was seen that they were looking better and had taken on more flesh than all the youths who ate at the king's rich dainties.* (Daniel 1:15 AMPC)

The Bible tells us that these young men were far superior to all others. They found favor with men, and gained wisdom and knowledge from God. What a winning combination! Despite the fact that he had been physically conquered, Daniel let the Word of God make him the victor!

Pray and Believe!

When our son Mike was six years old, a mentally disturbed woman kidnapped him from a playground. It was a very frightening experience! At the very moment we realized what had happened, my husband grabbed my hand to pray. He said, "Marilyn, we're going to believe that Mike will be safely returned to us in one hour." The police told us they had a report of a woman taking a little boy from the playground. We met a policeman at the playground. I looked down the street alongside the playground, and three blocks away I saw a woman walking with a small boy.

I shouted, "That's our son." The policeman told us to wait, jumped into his car, drove down to pick up Mike and the woman, and returned with our son. When Mike climbed out of the police car, I looked at my watch—it had been exactly one hour! We prayed, instead of getting into fear, and God was faithful to hear and answer our prayers! You can do the same.

Prayer Conquers Fear

Prayer is an essential part of overcoming fear! The king had ordered all the "wise men" to be destroyed because no one had been able to interpret the king's dreams, but Daniel didn't panic. Instead, he called a prayer meeting:

Then Daniel went to his house and made the thing known to . . . his companions, So that they would desire and request mercy of the God of heaven concerning this secret, that Daniel and his companions should not perish with the rest of the wise men of Babylon. (Daniel 2:17–18 AMPC)

Prayer came naturally to Daniel. He prayed three times a day—first thing in the morning, at noon, and the last thing at night. (Christians should have a disciplined prayer life.)

When my late husband Wally was alive and leading our church, he initiated early morning prayer sessions at our church. He "selected" the 5 a.m. sessions for himself and me. As the alarm rang at 4:30 a.m., I could not imagine how I would ever make it. Yet, I knew that my husband and God wanted me to go.

I began to claim the scripture that God rewards those who diligently seek Him found in Hebrews 11:6—even at 5 a.m. in the morning. God rewarded us for our diligence—we saw literally hundreds and hundreds of answers to prayer that year. Wally also led a group in prayer every Monday evening, and the lives of many in our church were transformed as they followed his example of diligent intercession.

As a result of prayer, God gave Daniel revelation, and he was given the ability to interpret the king's dream. When the king saw the discernment and wisdom of Daniel, he promoted him, and Daniel, the slave, became one of the most powerful men in the kingdom:

Then the king promoted Daniel and gave him many great gifts, and he made him ruler over the whole province of Babylon and chief prefect over all the wise men of Babylon. (Daniel 2:48)

Daniel had circumstances in his life that could have driven him to despair and defeat: slavery, fear of death, separation from family and friends. Fear could have driven out Daniel's faith if he had allowed it to, but he stayed strong in his trust of the Lord.

Don't Let Go of the Word!

For the word of God is living and active. Sharper than any double-edged sword, it penetrates even to dividing soul and spirit, joints and marrow; it judges the thoughts and attitudes of the heart. (Hebrews 4:12 NIV)

You may not have recognized it, but fear is the greatest hindrance you can have. Regardless of what happens to you, however, you can be free of its clutches. Fear cannot continue to grip a person who stubbornly refuses to not let go of faith in God's Word. The Word is alive! Let it guide you to complete freedom from fear.

First, don't focus on your circumstances—focus on God's Word. By looking at God, you will be filled with faith. Repeat the Word, say it over and over, and you will replace fear with God's truth (see Philippians 1:14).

Next, begin to praise God. Thank Him for His goodness and worship Him. Give a *"sacrifice of praise"* (Hebrews 13:15) in the midst of your terrible circumstances. Say, "Lord, I praise and thank You that I'm victorious, delivered, and set free. I thank You that all my needs are met *"according to His riches in glory in Christ Jesus"* (Philippians 4:19). Praising God will overcome fear (see Psalm 27).

Then act: do what you know God wants you to do. Is there something God told you to do, or something you vowed to do?

Then do it! It may be something as simple as not murmuring. If so, just quit! Whatever God tells you to do, act on the Word—do it! (See James 1:22–25.)

Finally, confess that you are delivered now! Pray the Word and believe in the answer. As Jesus said to Jairus, the synagogue ruler that had asked Jesus to heal his daughter, *"Do not be afraid; only believe"* (Mark 5:36 NKJV).

FAITH WILL OVERCOME FEAR... YOUR FREEDOM AND VICTORY ARE HERE!

STEPS TO BELIEVING BIG

1.

Look in a Bible concordance and write down three
verses that say we can *"put the enemy to flight."*

_____

_____

_____

2.

"Perfect love casts out fear." (1 John 4:18)
Recall times in your past when the love of God, or
others, delivered you from a fearful situation.
Share these times with a friend.

3.

Look at these four types of fear and find
scriptures to help you overcome them:

Fear of physical illness _____

_____

_____

Fear of physical circumstances_____

_____

Fear of man _____

_____

_____

_____

Fear of the world around you _____

_____

_____

_____

4.

Find godly people who have the boldness to do
what God has called them to do. Ask how God has
helped them overcome fear.

5.

Daniel is a great example of a godly person with high
morals and strong character. List five attributes of his
character (found in the book of Daniel) that you would
like to have. Pray, ask, and believe God for them.

_____

_____

_____

_____

_____

_____

_____

_____

_____

_____

_____

_____

6

TRIUMPH OVER TESTS, TRIALS, AND TEMPTATIONS

Blessed is the one who perseveres under trial because, having stood the test, that person will receive the crown of life that the Lord has promised to those who love him. (James 1:12 NIV)

Are you believing God for a provision or miracle in some area of your life, yet feel as though you are walking on hot coals to get to it? Most of us don't like to think about having to go through a test or trial, but chances are, you are in one right now! I've been through tests and I expect to go through many more.

There is a principle here you need to understand: God only promotes you when you successfully complete the present grade level. God wants to give you a miracle, but you can't get impatient and skip a level; you must believe that He will bring you through. Plus, He'd like you to face the test with joy:

My brethren, count it all joy when you fall into various trials, knowing that the testing of your faith produces patience. But let patience have its perfect work, that you may be perfect and complete, lacking nothing. (James 1:2–4 NKJV)

"Count it all joy?" To be totally honest, it's not always easy for me to be joyful in the middle of a trial. It's worth the effort, though, because when you are attacked by trials and temptations you can take joy in knowing there is a miracle just around the corner. Believe it or not, joyful praise is your strongest weapon! God wants your first response to hardships in life to be joy, because you need its strength to make it through and get your miracle: *"... Do not be grieved, for the joy of the LORD is your strength"* (Nehemiah 8:10).

You will overcome trials and temptations by praising the Lord, speaking the Word, and praying in the Spirit. These are the ways to practice your victory! When you praise, you will be encouraged to *fight*, walk in *faith*, and *stand* until you see your miracle:

Sing praise to the LORD, you His godly ones, and give thanks to His holy name.... Weeping may last for the night, but a shout of joy comes in the morning. (Psalm 30:4–5)

You're Stronger Than You Think

For whatever is born of God overcomes the world; and this is the victory that has overcome the world—our faith. (1 John 5:4)

Remember how God has brought you through hard times? "Rehearse" your victories of faith. As your faith is tested, you will learn to endure, and that brings maturity: *"knowing that the testing of your faith produces endurance"* (James 1:3). "Endure" means "to remain firm under suffering or misfortune without yielding; to bear patiently." *Endurance* is "the ability to withstand hardship or adversity."

Testing will prove and improve your faith—every time you take a God-kind-of-step in your trial, you become stronger. God doesn't want you to fail.

And let endurance have its perfect result, that you may be perfect and complete, lacking in nothing. (James 1:4)

There are many different kinds of trials, temptations, and tests. A trial can test your faith in God's Word. Take the Word *into* the trial and you'll become victorious *every time*. When you face a trial in your own strength, you may be tempted to give up, but stick with the Word and you can learn to overcome.

Have you ever gone hiking in the mountains and had your foot slip and slide back down the path? You can also "slip" in your faith and fail to trust God in a trial. Be encouraged—the Word says, *"My foot stands on a level place"* (Psalm 26:12). When you stand on His Word, you are safe and secure.

Once, when our ministry was going through a terrible financial trial, the devil told me to close the doors. He said that I had never been capable of making good financial decisions—that I had blown it. God didn't say that to me; in fact, God gave me a promise that if I would trust Him, He would bring me through. While my staff was worried, I stood on the Word. I said, "God will deliver us, God is delivering us," and within one month, *we had a total financial turnaround.* When the road ahead looks impossible, put your confidence in God and His Word: it will keep you steady—until circumstances come in line with God's Word.

The Big Three—Tests, Trials, and Temptations

"Tests," "trials," and "temptations" are three words translated interchangeably in different versions of the Bible. No one wants to go through hard times, but coming out the other side of a trial in victory demonstrates God's grace and power.

In the Old Testament, the root word for "test" is *tsaraph* meaning "to refine, try, melt, purge, try [test]."

Tsaraph also refers to "refinement by means of suffering." *"For You, O God, have tested us; You have refined us as silver is refined"* (Psalm 66:10 NKJV).

Peirazo is another root word used in the New Testament meaning "to tempt"; and in the Old Testament, *nacah* is a root word meaning "to test, to prove, to tempt, to try."

Learn Your Lessons

Submit yourselves, then, to God. Resist the devil, and he will flee from you. Come near to God and he will come near to you.
(James 4:7–8 NIV)

Like a mean classroom bully, Satan's purpose is to make you doubt the goodness of God by mocking you, tempting you, making you feel stupid, and causing you to doubt God. If you fill your mind with the Word, the temptation will seem like nothing more than a bully's blustering. Each test offers an opportunity to prove to yourself, the world, and the devil that you've learned your lesson: God's Word really does work! Even if you *feel* defeated, stand up and tell Satan that the game is not over—you are playing until you *win!*

Some fiery attacks from the devil are clearly designed to destroy your life and ministry. However, the water of God's Word will quickly put out the fire:

> *In addition to all, taking up the shield of faith with which you will be able to extinguish all the flaming arrows of the evil one.* (Ephesians 6:16)

> *No temptation has overtaken you but such as is common to man; and God is faithful, who will not allow you to be tempted beyond what you are able, but with the temptation will provide the way of escape also, so that you may be able to endure it.* (1 Corinthians 10:13)

Go to God

The word "stronghold," as used in the Bible, means "any fortified place" where you are not letting God teach and change you. Many times, we have deliverance, but the same problem returns time after time because we did not totally destroy the hold of sin over

> **The word "stronghold," as used in the Bible, means "any fortified place."**

a place in our lives and replace it with a fortress of God's Word.

We can be like yo-yos, going up and down between victory and defeat, fighting the same battle over and over—constantly repeating the same test. You don't have to live that way. You can live in continuous freedom:

So Jesus was saying to those Jews who had believed him, "If you continue in My word, then you are truly disciples of Mine; and you will know the truth, and the truth will make you free." (John 8:31–32)

For though we live in the world, we do not wage war as the world does. The weapons we fight with are not the weapons of the world. On the contrary, they have divine power to demolish strongholds. We demolish arguments and every pretension that sets itself up against the knowledge of God, and we take captive every thought to make it obedient to Christ. (2 Corinthians 10:3–5 NIV)

Get a Passing Grade

Since the children have flesh and blood, he too shared in their humanity... Because he himself suffered when he was tempted, he is able to help those who are being tempted.
(Hebrews 2:14, 18 NIV)

Even Jesus was tested: *"The Pharisees and Sadducees came up, and testing Jesus, they asked Him to show them a sign from heaven"* (Matthew 16:1) In another instance in which they tried to trap Him, *"... Jesus perceived their malice, and said, 'Why are you testing Me, you hypocrites?'"* (Matthew 22:18). These tests were obviously not from God, but because of them, Jesus is able to help us pass ours! How did Jesus resist temptation? His secret weapon was the Word of God.

I believe that God allows tests to come, but He never brings anything that you can't handle. The story of Abraham and Isaac shows how God wanted to "prove" Abraham—to test his faith. God asked Abraham to sacrifice his son—the son through whom God's promise would be fulfilled. Abraham never flinched—he offered his son Isaac and God saw his heart: *"Now it came about after these things, that God tested Abraham, and said to him, 'Abraham!' and he said, 'Here I am'"* (Genesis 22:1).

"... Now I know that you fear God, because you have not withheld from me your son, your only son." Abraham looked up and there in a thicket he saw a ram caught by its horns. He went over and took the ram and sacrificed it as a burnt offering instead of his son. So Abraham called that place The LORD *Will Provide.* (Genesis 22:12–14 NIV)

Listen to the "Teacher"

Let no one say when he is tempted, "I am being tempted by God"; for God cannot be tempted by evil, and He Himself does not tempt anyone. But each one is tempted when he is carried

away and enticed by his own lust…Do not be deceived, my
beloved brethren. (James 1:13–14, 16)

You can dwell on your temptations and entertain them. Even your personal plans, the desires of your heart, your own self-efforts can be lust or sin, if you haven't heard from God. You must resist the devil and become a "doer" of the Word:

> *Do not merely listen to the word, and so deceive yourselves. Do*
> *what it says. Anyone who listens to the word but does not do*
> *what it says is like someone who looks at his face in a mirror*
> *and, after looking at himself, goes away and immediately*
> *forgets what he looks like. But whoever looks intently into*
> *the perfect law that gives freedom, and continues in it—not*
> *forgetting what they have heard, but doing it—they will be*
> *blessed in what they do.*
> (James 1:22–25 NIV)

Adam and Eve, in the garden of Eden, had the first big test: *"Now the serpent was more crafty than any beast of the field which the* LORD *God had made"* (Genesis 3:1). Satan whispered to Eve, flattered her, and she listened—a big mistake! Then Adam listened to Eve. By the time Satan was finished, he had persuaded both of them to doubt God.

Watch out! Satan will use the same tactics on you. When you are at a crossroad to your miracle, Satan will whisper: "Are you sure God really wants you to do that? Did God really say that He would provide all your needs?" Don't listen to the devil. *Listen to God's Word!*

It's Just Another Test

*For no matter how many promises God has made, they are
"Yes" in Christ. And so through him the "Amen" is spoken by us
to the glory of God. Now it is God who makes both us and you
stand firm in Christ ... guaranteeing what is to come.*
(2 Corinthians 1:20–22 NIV)

Have you ever confessed the Word, rebuked the devil, done all
the right things, and waited ... waited ... and waited ... for the
manifestation of the promise, yet nothing happened? At these
times, you can hold on and keep believing God's promise or give
up and believe a lie.

My advice: hold on to your confession, hope against hope, and
continue to believe the promise that God will see you through.
Keep His Word in your mouth and you will see the fulfillment of
the promise. Do not walk by what you see; walk by faith.

It is easy to fall into the trap of taking matters into your own
hands. Have you ever tried to "help" God out and missed your
miracle? I have! Waiting for the promise can make you wonder if
it was even in God's plan in the first place. Rest assured, if God
makes a promise in His Word it is His will. However, your answer
can be delayed by spiritual opposition. God often sends angelic
warriors to deliver your answers:

*"Do not be afraid, Daniel. Since the first day that you set
your mind to gain understanding and to humble yourself
before your God, your words were heard, and I have come
in response to them. But the prince of the Persian kingdom*

resisted me twenty-one days. Then Michael, one of the chief princes, came to help me, because I was detained there with the king of Persia." (Daniel 10:12–13 NIV)

Choose Door Number Three

Children who fail in school sometimes have to repeat the same grade. Diligent teachers can hold them back for a purpose: they want the student to learn the material and be successful. Likewise, God is a diligent teacher and He will keep us traveling along the same roads until we learn the lesson!

The children of Israel went through numerous trials, failing one test after another. Why? Perhaps they couldn't learn to speak words of praise instead of complaint. When they crossed the Red Sea, the people were jubilant, filled with faith and trust in God. Soon, however, they had a new test: lack of water. They should have responded in faith, "If God can part the Red Sea, He can easily supply water for us." Instead, they murmured and complained, questioning Moses and God. Despite their bad attitudes, God honored Moses's prayers and turned the bitter waters of Marah into sweet water; at the next stop, He provided 12 springs of water and 70 date palms (see Exodus 15:23–27).

In the next chapter of Exodus, we read that the children of Israel went through another trial: lack of food. They could have said, "Our God just supplied abundant water for us, so we know He will provide food!" Instead, they complained. Does that sound like you? Are you wandering in a wilderness of trials and tribulations? Are you complaining and testing God? The Israelites *could* have been in the promised land in less than a year. Instead the Lord said to Moses:

"I have pardoned them according to your word"... yet [they] *have put Me to the test these ten times and have not listened to My voice,* [they] *shall by no means see the land which I swore to their fathers.* (Numbers 14:20–23)

What went wrong? They had a bad attitude and their problems overwhelmed them. You will either defeat your problems or they'll defeat you. You chose how you face a test: (1) complain, and take the test over again; (2) complain, *give up,* and totally miss God's promises and provision; OR (3) praise God, stand on His Word, pass the test, and enter the promised land! Wouldn't you rather pick door number three?

The True or False Quiz

Sometimes, while you are waiting for the provision of God during a trial, Satan will offer you a *counterfeit* answer. It can look *pretty good,* but not be *quite* in line with the Word. Beware: God will never go against His Word. Don't fail this easy quiz by falling for the schemes of the enemy. Be patient and wait for the *real* answer. Study God's Word for your situation and find out what He has to say. Better yet, read through the Bible every year and you will have a steady supply of Word to support you during any trial.

Long ago, Abraham fell for a counterfeit provision. God had promised him an heir, a son, but Sarah did not conceive, and they became impatient. Then Sarah suggested that Abraham have a son with Hagar, her Egyptian maid. Ishmael was born, but he was not the child of promise—he was a counterfeit! Although Ishmael was blessed in many ways, he was not the true heir. In due time,

God did provide the fulfillment of His promise to Abraham, and Isaac was born (see Genesis 16 and 21).

Practice Makes Perfect

Therefore there is now no condemnation for those who are in Christ Jesus. For the law of the Spirit of life in Christ Jesus has set you free from the law of sin and of death. (Romans 8:1–2)

God says your past failures are forever forgotten—you are free from attacks on your mind and character! You live under a higher law, the law of Spirit and life! Overcome every temptation by setting your mind on godly things. You don't have to live with guilt or self-pity or fall prey to Satan's lies about you. Sin has no power over you and neither does temptation. Temptation is not sin—as long as you resist it.

> **God says your past failures are forgotten forever.**

Purpose in your heart to give the Holy Spirit complete control of your life, He will always help you overcome temptation and live a life of peace:

For those who are according to the flesh set their minds on the things of the flesh, but those who are according to the Spirit, the things of the Spirit. For the mind set on the flesh is death, but the mind set on the Spirit is life and peace.
(Romans 8:5–6)

Fight the Bully

*But if the Spirit of Him who raised Jesus from the dead
dwells in you, He who raised Christ Jesus from the dead will
also give life to your mortal bodies through His Spirit
who indwells you.* (Romans 8:11)

Don't let Satan, the classroom bully, tell you that you can't accomplish your purpose—that you are a loser. Remind him that you have divine energy and ability. Satan will try to deceive you by saying, "You're too sickly, too stupid, too weak, or too old to do that. You might as well give up the fight." When you are filled with the Holy Spirit, He makes your body healthier and more energetic than it has ever been.

Also, remember who your real dad is: your position as a child of God entitles you to go to the "head of the class"! Get an image of yourself as a lawful heir to good things, then claim your inheritance! The Holy Spirit Himself will tell you who you are:

*For those who are led by the Spirit of God are the children of
God... And by him we cry, "Abba, Father." The Spirit himself
testifies with our spirit that we are God's children.*
(Romans 8:14–16 NIV)

One time, when we were going through some hard trials and I was very tired, the devil spoke to me, "You are having a nervous breakdown just like your father did. Why don't you just commit suicide right now?" That thought was so strong and overwhelming, I instantly cried out to God. "God, help me! Help me! I'm just like my father and I'm having a nervous breakdown!"

Just as quickly, the Lord spoke to me, "You *are* just like your Father, that's true. *I am* your Father—and *I've never* had a nervous breakdown, so you're not going to have one, either." If you allow God, He will deliver you from every trial:

> Because he has loved Me, therefore "I will deliver him; I will set him securely on high, because he has known My name. He will call upon Me, and I will answer him; I will be with him in trouble; I will rescue him and honor him." (Psalm 91:14–15)

Watch Your Language!

> "Woe to me," I [Isaiah] cried. "I am ruined! For I am a man of unclean lips, and I live among a people of unclean lips, and my eyes have seen the King, the Lord Almighty." (Isaiah 6:5 NIV)

God wants you to pay attention to how you talk. By saying negative words, you can fail your test! After King Uzziah died, Isaiah had a vision of God still on the throne, even though His people had hardened their hearts. Isaiah suddenly realized his mistake in speaking negatively and thought he had blown it. However, God gave him another chance and washed out his mouth. An angel went to Isaiah and touched his mouth with a live coal from the altar. His lips were cleansed, and his sins forgiven (see Isaiah 6:6–7).

You, too, may feel you have failed by speaking negative things—things contrary to God's Word—but have hope! You can change your words by refusing to utter the negative.

The Power of Prayer

A woman I knew was saved shortly after her husband's death, while her children were in their twenties. Her children were taking drugs and she was tormented with fear because they were all unsaved. It was a great trial to her, especially coming after her husband's death.

One night, as the woman was praying, God spoke to her and said, "Leave your children with me. It is my will to save them, so stop distressing yourself." From that night on, the mother never again worried about them. She stopped cooking up schemes to get them saved. She said, "They are God's problem." One morning at four o'clock, the mother was startled from sleep by a telephone call. It was her son, who said, "I have heard the voice of God. What should I do?" She led her boy to the Lord.

He became Spirit-filled, attended Bible college, and became an assistant pastor in Tulsa, Oklahoma. Today, every member of her family is saved because she allowed God to work in their lives rather than try to save them herself.

If the circumstances look bad after you pray, hang in there, God will work things out. This mother was patient and waited. She believed God's promise and received the reward!

It's a Fire Drill!

Shadrach, Meshach and Abednego replied to him, "King Nebuchadnezzar, we do not need to defend ourselves before you in this matter. If we are thrown into the blazing furnace, the God we serve is able to save us from it, and he will rescue us from Your Majesty's hand. But even if he does not, we want you to know, Your Majesty, that we will not serve your gods or worship the image of gold you have set up."
(Daniel 3:16–18 NIV)

These three young men were thrown into a fiery furnace because they would not serve a false god. They were determined to serve only the true God and to put their trust in Him. They spoke the right words and *lived*, despite the fire, because God was with them.

When fiery trials come against you, remember God's Word, speak it, and you too will be victorious. The fiery furnace was designed to terrorize the three Hebrew children into bowing to the golden idol. It didn't work. When they came out of the furnace, they didn't even smell of smoke. All the fire had done was burn up the ropes that bound them and burn to a crisp the soldiers who threw them into the fire.

You Have a Tutor—the Holy Spirit

In the same way the Spirit also helps our weakness; for we do not know how to pray as we should, but the Spirit Himself intercedes for us with groaning too deep for words; and He who searches the hearts knows what the mind of the Spirit is, because He intercedes for the saints according to the will of God. (Romans 8:26–27)

Facing trials and temptations on your own is daunting—that is why God gave you a helper—the Holy Spirit. Praying in the Spirit will give you a special power boost; plus, it reminds you that you need never go through your trials *alone.*

The Holy Spirit prays for you according to God's perfect will. In the midst of a test or trial, you can be so flustered and upset you can't think straight; sometimes you don't even have a clue how to pray, but *"the Spirit Himself intercedes for us."* Rest assured that everything will work together for good, just as God said it would!

Prayer is an excellent weapon against temptation. As you join in faith with God, you become part of a dynamic duo: *"You are from God, little children, and have overcome them; because greater is He who is in you than he who is in the world"* (1 John 4:4).

Bring Home the Prize

Let us throw off everything that hinders and the sin that so easily entangles. And let us run with perseverance the race marked out for us, fixing our eyes on Jesus, the pioneer and perfecter of faith.
(Hebrews 12:1–2 NIV)

Have you noticed that some Christians have a great victory, then immediately have a fierier trial? What happened? This can be a counterattack by Satan, but sometimes they have made something else their source instead of God and His Word. Be careful, if God isn't your source for everything, you are stepping into the devil's territory.

When you come through a temptation and trial (and you will), continue to build your place of victory. When you pull down the devil's strongholds, you must put strongholds (fortresses) of the Word in their place. There is a three-part plan, from the book of James, to neutralize an attack of the enemy.

Number One: Look ahead—*watch out* for "good-looking" bait with the hidden hook of sin. Consider that the consequence of sin is death and don't take the bait! *"Don't be deceived, my dear brothers and sisters"* (James 1:16 NIV).

Number Two: Look around—see and proclaim the goodness of God. He has provision for your every need. When you meet temptation say, "Why give in to that trap? God has much better things for me." He wants you to have a miracle!

> *Every good and perfect gift is from above, coming down from the Father of the heavenly lights, who does not change like shifting shadows.* (James 1:17 NIV)

Number Three: Look within—to the nature of Jesus Christ— see that you are clothed with His righteousness. When God looks at you, He says, "You are the best! You have my nature within."

> *He chose to give us birth through the word of truth, that we might be a kind of first fruits of all he created.* (James 1:18 NIV)

When you know a miracle is coming your way, suddenly the trial or test doesn't seem as difficult. Instead of giving into murmuring, speak the Word. During a trial, remember—God has prepared a miracle for the "outside," but He also wants to do a work on the "inside":

Knowing that the testing of your faith produces endurance. And let endurance have its perfect result, that you may be perfect and complete, lacking in nothing. (James 1:3–4)

God says, "Not only do I want to bring you a miracle, I also want to build your character." When you totally rely on the integrity of God's Word and trust Him in a trial, you will acquire maturity in your Christian walk. You must be patient, never diverting your eyes from what God has promised. Then you will become "perfect" or "complete" and lack for nothing

Who Will Condemn Us?

Who then will condemn us? Will Christ? No! For he is the one who died for us and came back to life again for us and is sitting at the place of highest honor next to God, pleading for us there in heaven.

Who then can ever keep Christ's love from us? When we have trouble or calamity, when we are hunted down or destroyed, is it because he doesn't love us anymore? And if we are hungry or penniless or in danger or threatened with death, has God deserted us?

Overwhelming victory is ours through Christ who loved us enough to die for us. For I am convinced that nothing can ever separate us from his love. Death can't, and life can't. The angels won't, and all the powers of hell itself cannot keep God's love away. Our fears for today, our worries about tomorrow, or where we are—high above the sky, or in the deepest ocean—nothing will ever be able to separate us from the love of God demonstrated by our Lord Jesus Christ when he died for us. (Romans 8:35-35, 37-39 TLB)

STEPS TO BELIEVING BIG

1.

Name some of the tests that came upon the children of Israel because of their lack of faith in God.

_____

_____

_____

_____

_____

2.

Think of a stronghold in your own life.
What Bible promises can you find to use as
a barrier against the lies of the devil?

_____

_____

_____

_____

_____

_____

_____

3.

List at least three positive ways you can
respond to a test or temptation.

_____

_____

_____

4.

What do "joy" and "patience" have to do with testing?
Do you know anyone who was joyful or patient
during a trial or test from whom you could learn?

_____

_____

_____

_____

_____

_____

_____

_____

_____

_____

5.

Meditate on James 1:16–18. Pray about how
to apply this truth to a trial you are facing.

7

USE YOUR GOD-GIVEN AUTHORITY

*And Jesus came up and spoke to them, saying, "All authority
has been given to Me in heaven and on earth."*
(Matthew 28:18)

What authority do you have in life? You may have *some* authority on your job, and you certainly should exercise authority over your children when they are young. Did you know you have been given great authority in this world?

If you have a problem with service in a restaurant, whom do you demand to see? If there's a mistake on your phone bill and customer service won't fix it, who will? When you are in a bind, when you really need to get something done, you ask for the "person in charge"—the person with authority.

When God created this world, He wanted mankind to be in charge of all creation.

Then God said, "Let Us make man in Our image, according to Our likeness; and let them rule over the fish of the sea and over the birds of the sky and over the cattle and over all the earth, and over every creeping thing that creeps on the earth." (Genesis 1:26)

It is amazing to consider that we were intended to "rule" the earth! In fact, God created this whole world for us:

The heavens are the heavens of the LORD, but the earth He has given to the sons of men. (Psalm 115:16)

God blessed them; and God said to them, "Be fruitful and multiply, and fill the earth, and subdue it; and rule over the fish of the sea and over the birds of the sky and over every living thing that moves on the earth." (Genesis 1:28)

God created Adam and Eve and told them to fill and subdue the earth. "Subdue" comes from the Hebrew word *kabash* which means "to conquer, subjugate, bring into bondage, force, keep under, bring into subjection." Just as man is subject to God's authority, creation is subject to man's authority:

You make him to rule over the works of Your hands; You have put all things under his feet. (Psalm 8:6)

God created the animals, but He *formed* man out of the existing earth and then breathed His life into him. When God created man and woman, He said they were "very good." Adam and Eve had

God's image, authority, and wisdom; their identities were in Him!

The good news is that God provided Adam with a perfect home, a beautiful wife, and a wonderful job taking care of a glorious garden!

The LORD God planted a garden toward the east, in Eden; and there He placed the man whom He had formed. (Genesis 2:8)

Adam had intelligence that surpasses anything we know today. He named all the animals and then remembered their names! He had perfect recall.

The bad news is that Satan could not stand the fact that God had given Adam authority over the world and its creatures. Satan wanted that authority for himself, so he planned to usurp it in order to become the "god of this world." He lied to Eve saying:

"For God knows that in the day you eat from it [the tree] *your eyes will be opened, and you will be like God, knowing good and evil."* (Genesis 3:5)

Don't Let Satan Steal Your Authority!

Wait a minute! God had already made Adam and Eve in His image. Adam and Eve had their authority, power, position—their identity—in God. Satan was tempting them to question their identity, just as he will try to make you question yours.

There are two things that Satan wants to take from you: the authority of God's Word and your identity in it. He wants to make you think that you are a nobody, alone and powerless. He wants you to act independently of God, without His authority. When Satan acted independently of God to gain his own authority, he lost it all. Now, he wants you to do the same thing. Man's authority is in God—not apart from Him!

Adam was given the authority to guard and protect the Garden: *"Then the LORD God took the man and put him into the garden of Eden to cultivate it and keep it"* (Genesis 2:15). Adam should have used his God-given authority to drive out the serpent, stop him from speaking contrary to God's Word, and warn his wife. By refusing to use his authority, he *lost* it!

Has Satan tried to play the same trick on you? Is the father of lies trying to convince you that you are a nobody? Have you begun to question whether God will really answer your prayers? Don't let Satan steal your authority!

Once I was on a plane going to Albany, New York, for a special church service. Before the plane departed, the pilot announced that we would be two hours late. My heart dropped, because if we were late, I would miss the service. Then the Lord spoke to me, "You know, you have authority in the name of Jesus." So, I began to bind the enemy from hindering the plane's departure. Within 15 minutes, the pilot said, "Well, it was not as big a problem as we thought, and we will be taking off shortly." We arrived in time for the service. The authority of Jesus is bigger than a delayed plane; it is bigger than any problem Satan can throw at you. Don't fall for the same deception that fooled Adam and Eve. You have been given authority over the devil by God Himself. Use it!

> You have been given authority over the devil!

Adam and Eve paid a terrible price for their mistake. They lost their dominion—the earth—by disobeying God. Though created in the image of God, Adam and Eve had taken on a strange, evil nature—that of sin. They lost their perfect home in the Garden and had to cultivate ordinary ground and work hard for everything they ate. They were barred from the Tree of Life, but worst of all, they had to leave the constant presence of God. Now, instead of walking and talking with Him intimately, they were reduced to worshiping Him with sacrifices from afar.

Power and Authority

Authority is largely a New Testament concept, infrequently seen in the Old Testament. The Hebrew word for "authority" is *toqeph* which means:

- Power
- Strength
- Energy

In the New Testament, the Greek word for "authority" is *exousia*. It has several meanings:

- Power of choice
- Physical or mental power
- Delegated authority in the form of a warrant, license, or authorization to perform
- The sphere in which authority is exercised.

God Promised a "Seed"

Satan was delighted. Now he had authority over mankind, whom he hated. Instead of ministering to God's creation (as he was created to do), he gained authority over creation. God saw this and cursed him.

> *And I will put enmity between you and the woman, and*
> *between your seed and her seed; he shall bruise you on the*
> *head, and you shall bruise him on the heel.* (Genesis 3:15)

This curse really shook up Satan. The "head" is a symbol of the authority he desired. God promised that, from the seed of Adam and Eve, a man would be born who would crush the devil and take back authority from him. The Old Testament gives the entire history of how the devil tried to prevent the seed of woman from reproducing for generation after generation until the birth of Jesus Christ.

Can Satan Destroy the Seed?

Satan didn't fully understand the promise of the seed, but he knew enough to start a campaign to destroy it. First, he saw that Abel's sacrifice was acceptable to God; therefore, he incited Cain to kill Abel, thinking that would cut off the seed.

When Satan heard about God's covenant with Abraham and his seed, he knew that seed had to be killed. He stirred up Esau to kill Jacob, thinking he was the promised seed. However, Jacob stood up in his newfound image as Israel (one who has prevailed with God and man) and found peace with his brother Esau.

Not knowing who the seed might be, the deceiver then enticed Pharaoh to order the murder of all male Hebrew babies; however, two parents named Amram and Jochebed stood up in their image of authority and managed to conceal their baby, saving him from certain death. Their son, Moses, became the deliverer.

> God promised that, from the seed of Adam and Eve, a man would be born who could crush the devil.

In the promised land, Satan heard that the seed was to come through David, so he attacked David's family line. A wicked woman named Jezebel caused the whole of Israel to follow after Baal. She arranged for her daughter, Athaliah, to marry a prince of the family of David and become the queen of Judah. Athaliah was as evil as Jezebel, and when her husband died, she had her son and all his heirs killed. Now surely the seed was destroyed—Satan thought he had won. Ah, but there was one little grandson, Joash, hidden away by Jehosheba, his aunt and a faithful woman married to a priest, Jehoiada. At the end of seven years, they brought Joash out, crowned him king, and killed Athaliah. Satan came very close to destroying all of David's seed, but failed.

During Israel's captivity, a decree was made by the Babylonian king, at the suggestion of Haman (inspired by Satan), to kill all the Jews in the land; but Queen Esther fasted and prayed for three days, went before the king, and saved the lives of the Jews! A Jewish queen of Babylon stood in her image of authority and saved her nation.

The Promise Fulfilled

Adam surrendered mankind's God-given authority to Satan, but God promised to restore that authority through Adam's seed. The best attempts of Satan, throughout the Old Testament, failed to destroy the seed; the New Testament is the celebration story of how Jesus, the seed, the new Adam, restored man's authority!

King Herod, stirred up by Satan to destroy the seed, ordered the murder of all male Jewish babies. But a man named Joseph stood up in his authority, obeyed God's voice, and hid baby Jesus in Egypt until King Herod died.

Satan missed again; the seed was not destroyed. Whenever men stand in their God-given authority, Satan is defeated. The seed, of course, is Jesus, the Son of God:

> *And after being baptized, Jesus went up immediately from the water; and behold, the heavens were opened, and he saw the Spirit of God descending as a dove, and lighting on Him, and behold, a voice out of the heavens, saying, "This is My beloved Son, in whom I am well-pleased."*
> (Matthew 3:16–17)

Satan must have known that Jesus was the seed and went after Him. In the wilderness, Satan tempted the Lord and said that if Jesus would worship him instead of God, Satan would give Him earthly authority. Jesus refused, knowing that His authority came from heaven, not earth. Jesus already knew who He was and the power He possessed.

Jesus knew that Satan had "official" authority over the world, which he received when the first Adam sinned. Jesus did not dispute Satan's ability to give Him the kingdoms of the earth during the temptation:

> *And he led Him up and showed Him all the kingdoms of the world in a moment of time. And the devil said to Him, "I will give You all this domain and its glory; for it has been handed over to me, and I give it to whomever I wish. Therefore if You worship before me, it shall all be Yours." Jesus answered and said to him, "It is written, 'YOU SHALL WORSHIP THE LORD YOUR GOD AND SERVE HIM ONLY'."* (Luke 4:5–8)

Jesus would not yield to Satan's authority, so Satan plotted to kill Him. Finally, the devil succeeded in killing Jesus, but that was all part of God's incredible plan! Death could not hold Jesus. He arose to complete God's plan to give authority back to man:

> *. . . That through death He might render powerless him who had the power of death, that is, the devil, and might free those who through fear of death were subject to slavery all their lives.* (Hebrews 2:14–15)

The Second Adam

How do we know that Jesus is the "second Adam," sent by God to restore man's authority? Let's look at the evidence. The second Adam must be a man, but He must also be without the sin nature. Jesus was born of a virgin through the Holy Spirit; therefore, the sin nature was not transferred to Him. There was no death in Jesus, only the life of God was in Him.

While the first Adam was disobedient to God, the second Adam had to be totally obedient. Jesus did only what the Father told Him, acting in complete harmony with the Father. He was obedient in everything, even to the point of dying on the cross! This obedience redeemed you and me!

> *For as through the one man's disobedience the many were made sinners, even so through the obedience of the One the many will be made righteous.* (Romans 5:19)

The first Adam was weak, falling to Satan's temptations. Jesus, the second Adam, was strong enough not only to resist Satan, but to defeat him completely, winning back mankind's lost authority.

> *The devil has sinned from the beginning. The Son of God appeared for this purpose, to destroy the works of the devil.* (1 John 3:8)

What are the works of Satan that Jesus must destroy? They are sin, sickness, poverty, and death.

Paralyze the Devil

> *Wherever He entered villages, or cities, or countryside, they were laying the sick in the market places, and imploring Him that they might just touch the fringe of His cloak; and as many as touched it were being cured.* (Mark 6:56)

Sickness does not come from God; it is a work of Satan. Jesus's authority is greater than Satan's, therefore, we can receive healing. Years ago, a staff member told me about her husband's horrendous back problem. I was unable to go and physically lay hands on him, and he was unable to come to church. So, I "sent the Word" to him in prayer and claimed this verse:

He sent His word and healed them, and delivered them from their destructions. (Psalm 107:20)

Early the next morning, I had to call his wife concerning another matter, and he answered the phone. He said, "The most unusual thing happened to me yesterday. Something clicked in my back while I was working. It went into place and I was healed. I slept like a baby all night." I asked him what time he was healed, and it was at the same time I had sent healing to him according to Psalm 107:20. Under God's authority, all things are possible.

Another work of Satan which Jesus destroyed was poverty; the devil seeks to impoverish people, ruin them, or put their focus solely on material things. God wants to give you power to gain wealth and then wants you to acknowledge where it came from:

But you shall remember the LORD your God, for it is He who is giving you power to make wealth, that He may confirm His covenant which He swore to your fathers, as it is this day. (Deuteronomy 8:18)

Jesus came to Earth and became poor so that we might become rich. He was not poor spiritually, but He was poor in regard to this world's goods, and the glory that He had with the Father. God gave us a firsthand example of how to prosper. He sowed His only Son and reaped millions of sons!

Jesus also destroyed the power of death. Death came upon all men because of the first Adam's sin, but the new Adam conquered death and took the sting out of it. *"O DEATH, WHERE IS YOUR VICTORY? O DEATH, WHERE IS YOUR STING?"* (1 Corinthians 15:55).

> **Jesus destroyed the power of death so that *you* would have that same authority in His name!**

This is one of Jesus's greatest victories. He was killed and descended into hell to defeat the evil one and claim everlasting life. He did this so that you would have power over death!

> *Therefore, since the children share in flesh and blood, He Himself likewise also partook of the same, that through death He might render powerless him who had the power of death, that is, the devil, and might free those who through fear of death were subject to slavery all their lives.* (Hebrews 2:14–15)

Finally, but most importantly, Jesus came to loose you from the hold of sin, defined as: "offend, trespass, to err, to miss the mark, and not share in the prize."

> *But now since you have been set free from the power of sin and have become the slaves of God, you have your present reward in holiness and its end is eternal life. For the wages which sin pays is death, but the [bountiful] free gift of God is eternal life*

through (in union with) Jesus Christ our Lord.
(Romans 6:22–23 AMPC)

Restoration of the Lost

Jesus's triumph on the cross restored the four things that Adam and Eve had lost: dominion over the earth, rights to the Tree of Life, ability to live in the image of God, and the hope of living forever in a perfect environment like the garden of Eden. Stop right now and meditate on this: Jesus defeated the devil, took authority over the earth, and then *gave that authority to you!*

Jesus has restored rightful dominion to those for whom it was first intended. All you have to do is believe in Him:

> *And Jesus came up and spoke to them, saying, "All authority has been given to Me in heaven and on earth."* (Matthew 28:18)

Jesus has made it possible for you to do His kind of work:

> *"Truly, truly, I say to you, he who believes in Me, the works that I do he will do also; and greater works than these he will do; because I go to the Father."* (John 14:12)

Have you ever needed to get a document signed by a person who couldn't physically be there to sign it? That person can give you the authority to handle legal matters in their name. Such authority is called "power of attorney." However, that person has to trust you before they'll give you the right to sign in their name! Jesus has given us power of attorney to do His work here on earth.

He is trusting you and me to represent Him.

Remember when Adam and Eve disobeyed God? They were cut off from the Tree of Life and God stationed cherubim and a flaming sword to guard it. Jesus has restored to you the Tree of Life—eternal life. The fruits of the Tree of Life are righteousness and fulfilled desires. Jesus made us righteous through His sacrifice, and *"The fruit of the righteous is a tree of life"* (Proverbs 11:30). He gives you the desire of your heart, and *"desire fulfilled is a tree of life"* (Proverbs 13:12).

We are restored to the image of God. Man was originally made in God's image, but when Adam fell into Satan's trap, he gave up his godly image for an evil one. Now Jesus has cleansed away that evil, so that we can once again reflect the glory of God.

Best of all, Jesus has purchased for you the right to enter a perfect environment. If the garden of Eden was wonderful, heaven is beyond our wildest wishes! (The home which Jesus prepares for us has no curse, no death, no tears, and no pain.) Can you imagine this incredible new earth, where God will physically be with us forever? When Jesus comes again to bring a new heaven and a new earth, there will again be the actual Tree of Life:

> *On either side of the river was the tree of life, bearing twelve kinds of fruit, yielding its fruit every month; and the leaves of the tree were for the healing of the nations.* (Revelation 22:2)

Claim Your Inheritance

I pray that the eyes of your heart may be enlightened, so that you will know what is the hope of His calling, what are the

riches of the glory of His inheritance in the saints.
(Ephesians 1:18)

So, you are in a tough spot—between a rock and a hard place: what are you going to do? *Take your position of authority!* As a child of God, Jesus has restored your inheritance. You are to *rule with Him.* However, Satan hasn't gotten the message yet. He is still fighting the battle, even though he has already lost the war.

If you are not taking authority over Satan, he is taking authority over you. Your physical and spiritual life, possessions, and family are all things that Satan would like to steal and destroy, but he has lost his power over you. Jesus has crushed the devil and you are to do the same thing:

> *For this reason also, God highly exalted Him, and bestowed on Him the name which is above every name, so that at the name of JESUS EVERY KNEE WILL BOW, of those who are in heaven, and on earth, and under the earth.* (Philippians 2:90–10)

I was once invited to speak at a large church in Cincinnati, Ohio. I arrived late at night with a number of boxes that contained my tapes and books. As I watched the boxes being removed from the luggage carrier, I noticed someone headed for the exit with a piece of luggage exactly like mine. I ran after the man and asked him if he had my luggage. He dropped the bag and ran. He had meant to steal it, but the Holy Spirit directed my attention to him so that my luggage could be recovered. The devil cannot steal from you if you will stand in the authority of Jesus's name!

Your inheritance is power and authority over the devil. God

wants you to experience this power! Notice, this power is for those who believe. If you don't believe that you reign with Jesus, if you don't stand in the image of God, it won't work. Get to know the power that you have in Christ, and then use it!

God . . . in these last days has spoken to us in His Son, whom He appointed heir of all things, through whom also He made the world. And He is the radiance of His glory and the exact representation of His nature, and upholds all things by the word of His power. (Hebrews 1:1–3)

Your Weapons of Warfare

You will not be able to enter into your position of authority without a battle. Fortunately, God has provided the armor you need to win (see Ephesians 6:14–17).

- The belt of truth
- The breastplate of righteousness
- The gospel of peace
- The shield of faith
- The helmet of salvation
- The sword of the Spirit

Notice that God provides the armor, but you have to put it on and use it!

He Is the Head

He is also head of the body, the church; and He is the begin-
ning, the firstborn from the dead, so that He Himself will come
to have first place in everything. (Colossians 1:18)

Jesus is the head and we are the body. How do your head and body get along? Your body follows where your head directs it! That is exactly what we are to be doing. As the body of Christ, we are called to do as He does.

Jesus is the head and He intercedes for the body. He sends power to the body. He sends the Holy Spirit to the body: *"... as Christ also is the head of the church, He Himself being the Savior of the body"* (Ephesians 5:23).

As you look at Jesus, you begin to want to be like Him. Your nature changes to be more like His—you begin to intercede. You want to see the Word work, to see the Spirit work. Then Psalm 37:4 begins to come true in your life: *"Delight yourself in the LORD; and He will give you the desires of your heart."*

As you delight yourself in the Lord, your desires get in line with the one in whom you are delighting, and you receive not only what you want, but what He wants!

Some days life just seems too hard. Maybe you have even had weeks or months like that—days of discouragement that Satan used to draw your attention away from God's plan for your life. That is why it is vitally important for you to claim the authority of Jesus over your world. Don't allow the world to overcome you; you are to overcome the world. Affect the world wherever you go instead of letting the world affect and mold you.

For whatever is born of God overcomes the world; and this is
the victory that has overcome the world—our faith.
(1 John 5:4)

You can overcome the influences and evil of the world because
you have the greater one inside you, and you bear His image. That
image is an image of authority!

Your Areas of Authority

Suppose your boss said to you "I'm going on a trip. You take over
while I'm gone." You might be thrilled to be "the boss" for a while,
but before long you would begin to have questions about your
authority: "Can I write checks?" "Can I hire and fire people?"
"Should I make important decisions on my own?" Soon you would
be calling your boss to find out exactly what authority he/she had
left to you.

Like any good leader, Jesus made it *very clear* where your authority lies. First, you have authority over the influences of evil men
who rule over others. Next, you have authority over principalities,
powers, and demonic forces:

Behold, I have given you authority to tread on serpents and
scorpions, and over all the power of the enemy, and nothing
will injure you. (Luke 10:19)

You also have authority over affliction, sickness, and disease.
In all these things you are more than a conqueror because you are
supposed to win. You are to take authority over situations:

*These things speak and exhort and reprove with all authority.
Let no one disregard you.* (Titus 2:15)

Take authority over bad habits and things that threaten your faith. Let the Holy Spirit show you how:

*Do you not know that your body is a temple of the Holy
Spirit who is in you, whom you have from God, and that you
are not your own? For you have been bought with a price:
therefore glorify God in your body.* (1 Corinthians 6:19–20)

Although authority belongs to you the moment you are born again, to use it effectively, you must practice. Practice *using* the Word and *taking a stand* against the enemy. Satan will fight. He will not give up an inch of ground without a battle. Take Jesus's Word into the circumstances and you will have the victory God has planned for you!

STEPS TO REIGNING IN LIFE

1.

You rule through Jesus Christ (Romans 5:17).

2.

You live by keeping the Word in your mouth (Matthew 4:4).

3.

God crushes Satan under your feet (Romans 16:20).

4.

You claim your inheritance of power
(Ephesians 1:17–19).

5.

You take your seat with Christ in heavenly
places (Ephesians 2:5–7).

6.

You become a world overcomer (1 John 4:4).

7.

You receive your victory in faith (1 John 5:4).

STEPS TO BELIEVING BIG

1.

Think of a time in the last few days when you have given up your authority. What can you do now to reclaim it?

_____

_____

_____

_____

_____

_____

_____

2.

Jesus restored things that Adam and Eve lost in the Garden. Choose one of them and explain to a friend how it has been personally restored to you.

3.

Write down some biblical examples of your God-given power to "reign in life."

_____

_____

_____

_____

_____

_____

_____

4.

Pray for a greater revelation of your authority
when using the name of Jesus. List three
things you should do in that name.

_____

_____

_____

_____

_____

_____

_____

5.

Meditate on the verses in Ephesians 6:14–17
and practice putting on the armor of God.
Relate to a friend how that armor protects
you and how it could protect them!

GOD
PROMISED THAT,
FROM THE
SEED OF ADAM
AND EVE,
A MAN
WOULD BE
BORN WHO
COULD CRUSH
THE DEVIL.

CHAPTER

8

FAITH THAT GETS PRAYERS ANSWERED

Then Jesus said to her, "O woman, your faith is great; it shall be done for you as you wish." And her daughter was healed at once. (Matthew 15:28)

In this chapter, I'm going to show you an important ingredient of God-like faith, the faith that *always gets what it asks of God!* During a trip that took Jesus beyond the border of Israel, He found a woman with "great" faith.

Before you say, "I could never have that kind of faith," you need to understand that you and I would never have called this person a "woman of great faith." She didn't know Jesus very well; probably, she had never read the Bible or even been to church; she wasn't a member of the chosen race; the disciples tried to get rid of her; and even Jesus seemed to treat her rudely. Like a lot of us, she seemingly had nothing going for her. In spite of all that, her prayer was answered and Jesus Himself announced to the world that this was a *woman of great faith*. You can do what she did and get what she got—her prayers answered—when you never, never, never give up!

Never, Never, Never Give Up!

During World War II, as English cities and towns were being bombed daily, Winston Churchill wanted to encourage the English people. Their homes were being destroyed and their friends and neighbors were dying; the Nazis seemed to be winning the war. What could Churchill say to his people in these terrible circumstances? He sent one clear message: "Never, never, never give up!"

Often, when times seem the darkest and our prayers are unanswered, we want to give up. People might think we're foolish to keep praying and believing when we aren't seeing results. Some might even blame us for the situation, believing that if we had done things *their* way, everything would be all right. Don't take the criticism to heart. Great faith never, never, never gives up!

There are many wonderful examples of passionate faith in the Bible. The Canaanite woman in Matthew 15 is a perfect example of someone who persisted against the odds. She came to Jesus with a hopeless situation, but great faith.

This woman's daughter was suffering terribly from demon possession—perhaps wracked by convulsions and delusions as she was being consumed by the devil. When her mother heard that Jesus had come to town, she went out to Him, fully trusting that He *could* heal her child.

Here are the first two conditions for *answered* prayer: first, the Canaanite woman had a *need*; second, she believed Jesus *could meet* that need. Before you go to God, search your heart. Be sure you truly believe that He can, and will, provide.

This woman was a gentile, one of the "accursed race" who had no right to approach Jesus—so she called out to Him from a distance, "Lord, Son of David, have mercy on me!" (See Matthew 15:22.) Imagine her agony over her daughter's condition. Her cry must have been loud, anguished, heartbreaking. Yet, Jesus ignored her!

Rejected by Jesus?

When I first read this story, I almost couldn't believe it! How could our gracious and loving God have ignored such a desperate cry for help? This woman wasn't even asking for herself, but for her daughter. She was unselfish, respectful, and full of faith. Still, Jesus ignored her! Sometimes, we may feel that God is treating us the same way. We plead, "Lord, you know how much I need this. I've come to you in complete faith. I'm not even asking this for myself. Why aren't you answering me?" The Canaanite woman *surely* felt discouraged, *but*—she never gave up!

If being ignored by Jesus wasn't hard enough, the disciples rejected her, too. "Send her away," they said. "She is really annoying."

You have to be persistent in your faith.

Have you ever been treated poorly by believers or even pastors or Christian leaders? Have you been looked down upon, perhaps told that your prayers are ineffective, or that you don't have enough faith? Criticism can make you want to give up.

Imagine God's chosen ministers waiting to be rid of this Canaanite woman! They seemingly had no compassion. Because she didn't fit the profile of a person to whom they were called to minister, they "discarded" her. Would you give up on God's healing if a pastor or evangelist was abrasive or rude to you concerning your healing? This woman didn't! She knew why she was there. She refused to have her faith denied.

What happens next is incredible. *"He [Jesus] answered, 'I was sent only to the lost sheep of Israel'"* (Matthew 15:24 NIV). That was a real shocker! Healing was for the Jews, but not for her. Have you ever felt that healing was for a certain select few, but not for you? Someone may have even told you that. Notice this woman didn't simply accept rejection and go away angry or defeated. That's exactly what most of us would have done. Instead, she got even closer to Jesus. She knelt before Him, worshiped Him, and asked Him again, *"Lord, help me!"* (Matthew 15:25 NIV).

Jesus had ignored and rejected her. What He did next seemed even worse. He replied,

"It is not right to take the children's bread and toss it to the dogs" (Matthew 15:26 NIV).

Man's Best Friend

Dogs are frequently mentioned in Scripture. They were used by the Hebrews to guard their houses and flocks. Packs of hungry, semi-wild dogs wandered about the fields and streets of the cities, eating garbage and fighting among themselves. In Psalm 22:16–20, fierce and cruel enemies are called dogs. Because the dog was an unclean animal, people would call themselves "dogs" to indicate their failings and to humble themselves.

Reading this statement over and over again, I had to wonder, "Did Jesus actually call this woman a dog?" How insulting! Then I studied His words more closely and realized that Jesus was not being insulting at all. He knew exactly what He was saying; the "children" were the children of Israel, and their "bread" was Jesus, the Bread of Life. The Jews often called the gentiles "dogs." Although most Jews rejected Jesus, some gentiles received Him.

The Proud Receive Nothing

Out of her faith, this woman answered Jesus's challenge. She didn't claim to have a right to the bread of the children; she asked for their crumbs! Isn't that amazing? She could have puffed up with pride and said, "I am every bit as good as any Jew!" Instead, she humbled herself, *"Even the dogs eat the crumbs that fall from their master's table"* (Matthew 15:27 NIV).

She recognized her unworthiness; she would settle for crumbs, knowing that even the crumbs of Jesus's love would be enough! Jesus's plan for this strange conversation was perfect. His apparent harshness brought out her passionate faith.

To be effective in prayer and honest before God, we must come to Him in humility. Which prayers most impress God? The ones from people who say, "I am a good Christian. I go to church every week and I read my Bible. I am better than most of the people around me, so I expect You to answer my prayer." Or the ones from people who say, "Lord, I can do nothing at all without You. I don't deserve Your love and compassion, but I totally depend on You"?

Have you ever felt that Jesus wasn't listening when you prayed or that He was refusing to help you? It may have seemed that way to this Canaanite woman, but she refused to leave without her miracle. Jesus loved her persistence and knew all along that He was going to help her daughter if she persisted. He had compassion for her, but He also had a point to make about faith: even when you feel like you've been ignored or turned down in prayer, keep asking and keep believing the way the Canaanite woman did. What was the result of her persistence?

> *Then Jesus said to her, "O woman, your faith is great; it shall be done for you as you wish." And her daughter was healed at once.* (Matthew 15:28)

Before Jesus came to the Canaanite woman's hometown, He had spoken with some Pharisees and teachers from Jerusalem (see Matthew 15:1–20). He called them "hypocrites," and headed off to Tyre and Sidon, a region inhabited by gentiles— a place He had compared to Sodom and Gomorrah! This was one of the only times that Jesus left the border of Israel! He left His "children," who rejected Him, and went to the region of the gentiles.

I believe He went there solely for this woman and her need. Christ had come as bread or manna for His children, but they rejected Him. The Bread of Life was brushed off the table, and when it broke into crumbs, a satisfying portion went to this gentile woman. He was not ignoring, rejecting, or insulting her—He was reaching out to meet her every need, because He loved her and because she never, never, never gave up.

The timing of Jesus's answers to our prayers can prepare us for victory. Don't walk away when you think that He is rejecting you.

Instead, keep on worshiping and trusting Him and passionately believing that He will give you the answers to prayer that you need.

Practice Makes Perfect

Christ told the Canaanite woman, *"O woman, your faith is great"* (Matthew 15:28).

What steps did she take to practice great faith?

- She came to Christ when the situation was hopeless.
- She persisted when her prayer seemed to be denied.
- She still pleaded when obstacles were presented.
- She waited at the feet of the Lord for His mercy.

Don't "Knock" Knocking

One day, the disciples asked Jesus to teach them how to pray. He taught them the "Lord's Prayer" and then continued with this story. A man welcomed an unexpected late-night visitor but had no bread to serve his guest. The man went to a neighbor's house hoping to borrow three loaves. The neighbor was not happy about being disturbed in the middle of the night. "I can't get up and give you anything," he said, "We are already in bed!" Jesus explained:

Although he will not get up and supply him anything because he is his friend, yet because of his shameless persistence and insistence, he will get up and give him as much as he needs.

So I say to you, Ask and keep on asking and it shall be given you; seek and keep on seeking and you shall find; knock and keep on knocking, and the door shall be opened to you. For everyone who asks and keeps on asking receives; and he who seeks and keeps on seeking finds; and to him who knocks and keeps on knocking the door shall be opened.
(Luke 11:8–10 AMPC)

Jesus told another parable to illustrate His point. A widow seeking legal counsel went to a judge who neither feared nor respected God. Although the judge was unwilling to help her, she continued to bother him, Finally, he decided that if he didn't help her, she'd be at his doorstep *all the time* (see Luke 18:1–5). She was not willing to give up!

Jesus tells us that we can sometimes get results by simply knocking on the door. At other times, we must be persistent, bringing our request over and over before the throne of God. However, unlike the ungodly judge, God doesn't answer us just to get rid of us.

And the Lord said, "Hear what the unrighteous judge said; now will not God bring about justice for His elect, who cry to Him day and night, and will He delay long over them? I tell you that He will bring about justice for them quickly. However, when the Son of Man comes, will He find faith on the earth?"
(Luke 18:6–8)

God answers us out of love. He answers us because of our persistent faith in who He is—a compassionate and loving God who really cares about our needs. He just loves your consistency when you never, never, never give up.

Blind Faith—Big Benefits

Now let's look at the story of a man who could have given up before he started. Bartimaeus was both blind and poor—so poor that he was begging at the gates of Jericho. *Bartimaeus* means "son of the unclean," so Bartimaeus's father was apparently ill with perhaps a contagious disease. It would have been easy for Bartimaeus to say, "Well, my father was sick his entire life and I will be too," but he wasn't about to accept that excuse! He heard that Jesus of Nazareth was passing by, so he quickly called out, *"Jesus, Son of David, have mercy on me!"* (Luke 18:38). The people around him told him to be quiet. They were trying to listen to the Master, and they didn't want the blind man's cries to distract them. Bartimaeus was not discouraged. He passionately wanted his eyesight—and he knew Jesus could give it to him.

> *Those who led the way were sternly telling him to be quiet; but he kept crying out all the more, "Son of David, have mercy on me!"* (Luke 18:39)

At last, Jesus called for him. Bartimaeus was led to Jesus. Jesus asked him,

> *"What do you want Me to do for you?" And he said, "Lord, I want to regain my sight!" And Jesus said to him, "Receive your sight; your faith has made you well."* (Luke 18:41–42)

Bartimaeus received his miracle. It didn't matter if his father had been ill, or if he was as poor as a church mouse. He believed and never gave up—and received his sight. There's something even more important here. As soon as he received his sight, he began following Jesus. He left Jericho and traveled with Jesus. God is thrilled to answer our prayers when we respond by following Him in all we do and say.

Too often, when we have an unanswered prayer, we think we have to try harder, or be a "better" person. Yet, looking at the Canaanite woman and blind Bartimaeus, neither of them tried to earn the right to their prayer requests. They didn't say, "Hey Jesus, You have to do this for me because I am so good."

Look carefully at the Scriptures. Both of them asked first for mercy! They were saying, "I can't earn this wonderful gift, Lord. I can't pay for it. The only way my prayer can be answered is through Your mercy, Your forgiveness, Your love." God wants us to acknowledge His Lordship, and to humble ourselves before Him. When we do this, His blessings flow and flow!

Prayer-A-Thon

Remember Daniel? He was burdened for his people. Two years had passed since the first group of Jews returned to Jerusalem. Daniel must have known his people were being harassed by their enemies. I think he longed to understand the destiny of the Jews, so he prayed and fasted for three weeks. Daniel was a man of prayer, accustomed to getting results! God had always answered him, given him wisdom, direction, and protection. This time Daniel prayed *non-stop* for three weeks. He was starting to ask, "How long, Lord?" Finally, the answer came! Notice that he didn't stop praying until He heard from God.

Then behold, a hand touched me and set me trembling on my hands and knees ... Then he said to me ... "Do not be afraid, Daniel, for from the first day that you set your heart on understanding this and on humbling yourself before your God, your words were heard." (Daniel 10:10, 12)

The Merciful God

Mercy actually defines our relationship with God! God truly wants a relationship with sinful mankind, but He must show us mercy in order for this relationship to be possible.

Our very salvation was achieved by God's mercy for us. Mercy is so essential to salvation that Paul refers to heirs of salvation as *"vessels of mercy"* (Romans 9:23) and those who fail to receive salvation *"vessels of wrath"* (Romans 9:22). Christ's life, death, and resurrection are God's ultimate display of mercy toward us.

When we are living in Christ, we are so overwhelmed with the gift of God's mercy that we want to share it with everyone—and we become models of God's mercy in this world.

We become channels of His mercy to the world through giving, volunteering, and helping the needy.

Ponder the wonder of God's mercy toward us. We did nothing to deserve such a gift. Having received it, our hearts are driven to pass on to others the wonderful gift of His love.

The Bible tells us that God's "princes" had to fight Satan's "princes," and that is why Daniel's answer took three weeks.

"I have come in response to your words. But the prince of the kingdom of Persia was withstanding me for twenty-one days; then, behold, Michael, one of the chief princes, came to help me . . ." (Daniel 10:12–13)

If you are praying consistently but not getting an answer, remember—there are powers of darkness in this world. Remember, too, that you have authority over these powers. They may *delay* your answers, but through persistence, you can refuse to be defeated!

Check Your Seed

We know that even when it seems that our prayers are not getting results, God hears us. When you have asked and asked and been persistent, it is time to ask yourself these questions:

First, "Am I walking in love toward my brothers and sisters and the world around me?" Faith works by love. If your faith isn't working, check your "love level." Remember, Paul told us that it is not our actions that get results, but our love.

For in Christ Jesus neither circumcision nor uncircumcision means anything, but faith working through love.
(Galatians 5:6)

Check your conversation. Are your words to and about others always loving? Check your prayers. Are they just about you and what you want, or are you praying in love for those around you? Take a special look at how you treat your family and friends. Sometimes we put great effort into helping strangers and forget to treat those closest to us with love and mercy.

Next, consider whether you are harboring unforgiveness.

Whenever you stand praying, forgive, if you have anything against anyone; so that your Father also who is in heaven may forgive you your transgressions. (Mark 11:25)

If we have unforgiveness in our hearts, our faith is hindered. If you truly want to know why your faith is not working, ask God to expose any remnants of unforgiveness.

Now, search your heart for jealousy or strife. Do you resent someone who has more wealth or success than you do? Are you competing with someone in your family, church, or workplace? Approach this question prayerfully, because often we cannot see our own envy and selfish ambition. Faith cannot flourish in an atmosphere of jealousy or rivalry. Root them out!

Next, be sure you're not operating in fear. As we have already learned, fear is the opposite of faith. When our actions are fear-driven, our faith is bound, and the results we get are not the ones we desire. If you are really trusting God, there is nothing to fear. Fear is not from God—take authority over it.

For God has not given us a spirit of timidity, but of power and love and discipline. (2 Timothy 1:7)

Finally—be sure you're focused on your harvest. If you want to grow beans, you have to *plant* beans. Check your "farming methods." If you are desiring to harvest souls for the Lord, have you planted the Word in their hearts? If you need help with finances, have you given to others so that you might receive? Are you lonely and need friendship? Have you been a friend to others? Sometimes we have a crop failure because we didn't plant anything! The God-kind of faith is working faith that plants as well as reaps.

Mind Your Motives

Sometimes the motives behind our request are not really based on faith, but on fleshly desire. We want something because it appeals to us, so we ask the Lord for it. As He says in James 4:3:

> *You ask and do not receive, because you ask with wrong motives, so that you may spend it on your pleasures.*

We can ask things of God and yet fail to receive them when we ask with a wrong purpose or selfish motives.

We can have a fleeting, soulish thought, pray for something on the spur of the moment, and wonder why God doesn't answer. It was not a *conviction*; it was just a *whim*. Elijah was a great man of faith, but at one point he prayed to die (1 Kings 19:4). That was not faith talking—that was flesh—and God didn't answer Elijah's prayer.

When we know that we are asking according to God's will, we can ask with utmost confidence and faith—so, be honest with yourself and check your motive!

Doubt Your Doubts

But he must ask in faith without any doubting, for the one who doubts is like the surf of the sea, driven and tossed by the wind. For that man ought not to expect that he will receive anything from the Lord. (James 1:6–7)

When you bring your request to God, believe that He will answer you while you are praying! Drop those doubts, don't let them get in the way of your faith.

Therefore I say to you, all things for which you pray and ask, believe that you have received them, and they shall be granted you. (Mark 11:24)

A member of my Bible study group a few years back had a hip bone removed. She would have to stand at our group meetings because of the pain in her back, due to the missing bone.

One day, I taught on healing and it really made her angry. She said, "Doctors are for healing, Jesus is for your sins, and the two shall never meet." I showed her many, many scriptures that said Jesus Himself took our infirmities and our diseases, but that just made her more upset.

A few weeks later, a friend invited this woman to a miracle service. The pastor came down into the audience and said, "There are people here with severe back problems. If you will stand up, God is healing back problems right now." The friend urged the woman to stand up . . . until she finally did. She felt a warmth flow all over her body. Later that evening, as the woman was getting ready for bed, her daughter came into her room and said, "Mother, what is that on your hip? It looks like a hip bone," and her back pain was gone forever! Hallelujah!

God will help you with your doubts. Just take that first step. Stand up. Ask Him to remove the doubts and replace them with unwavering faith.

Feelings and Faith

Look inward—prayerfully—and ask God if you are substituting emotion for faith. When we hear the testimonies of others, our faith can get a spiritual lift. We soar to the mountaintop because someone else's experience has encouraged us. Testimonies of healing and miracles should reinforce our belief in God's Word and remind us of His faithfulness to fulfill it.

Testimonies are meant to encourage us, but they can never take the place of digging into God's Word and getting His promise for our situation firsthand. Testimonies of healing and miracles should drive us back to the Word—the origin of faith! Make sure you are asking with faith, not emotion. Be joyful over what God has done for others; praise Him for His wonderful works; say to yourself, "If God did it for them, He'll do it for me!" Then get into the Word for your own sustenance, blessing, and faith-building!

Who's Got Time?

Are you ready to give up? Is the answer to your prayer taking longer than you had hoped? If you have examined your heart for the characteristics of faith and know that you are praying "right," then keep trusting God. Satan might be delaying the answer, but it is on its way!

> *Wait for the LORD. be strong, and let your heart take courage; yes, wait for the LORD.* (Psalm 27:14)

God is never late, but He often seems to be last minute! Try setting your spiritual alarm clock. I have a friend who had a wart on her face. She set the alarm clock!

That afternoon, a man rang her doorbell. While she stood talking to him, the man said, "Lady, did you notice something fall off your forehead?" There on the ground was the wart! Put your trust in God's time. It is always perfect.

Have You Checked the Plans?

A builder doesn't just "slap" together a house. Before he lifts a bit of lumber, he checks the blueprints, then re-checks them many times during construction. He knows that if he fails to follow the plans, the house will be a failure. Check and re-check God's plan for your life.

One time, the Lord spoke to me and said, "You know, you should be believing for more miracles when you teach." I said "Lord, you called me to be a teacher, you didn't call me to move in miracles. I don't see in the Bible where teachers move in miracles."

It is not enough to teach the Word; I must believe for the miraculous.

God pulled me up short and reminded me of the man that came to Jesus by night, and said to Him:

"Rabbi, we know that You have come from God as a teacher; for no one can do these signs that You do unless God is with him." (John 3:2)

God showed me that it is not enough to teach the Word; I must also believe for the miraculous. The more I believe for miracles, the more miracles God does.

Do you know what God's specific call on your life is? Obey that call and get your faith in line with that call. Go back to the Word again and again to be sure you are building the life God designed. If God has called you to work with youth on Saturday nights, then don't pray for a job that conflicts with that. God is able to give you a job that leaves you free to do His work. God wants your life to harmonize with His will, and He will not answer prayers that are inconsistent with His plan for your life.

At times, your prayers will be answered instantly. At other times, you will need to be persistent. "Ask, "seek," "knock" until you have God's answer to your situation. You may be puzzled about why others get answers while you're still waiting. Check your heart—including motives, your love walk, and any leftover fear or strife. Make sure there are no roadblocks that you have put up which prevent God from answering your prayers. When God shows you areas in your life that need to be changed, *change them.* Be repentant and obedient. No matter what has happened in the past—whatever person, teacher, or system has failed you—God never has and never will fail! You can completely trust in Him. Passionate faith pleases God and gets results.

IT IS NOT ENOUGH TO TEACH THE WORD; I MUST BELIEVE FOR THE MIRACULOUS.

STEPS TO BELIEVING BIG

1.

Write down three times in your life
when faith resulted in blessings.

_____

_____

_____

2.

Think about any obstacles to your faith such as fear,
envy, doubt, or wrong motives. Ask God, through
His Word, to show you how to combat them.

3.

Write down your most urgent or important
prayer request. Now list the seed that you have
planted in preparation for your harvest.

Prayer Request_____

Seed Planted_____

4.

For three days, write down on a single piece of
paper every word of doubt that comes out of
your mouth. Then take that piece of paper and
throw those words of doubt in the trash!

5.

Find an example in Scripture for each of the following:

**Someone who waited a long time
for an answer to prayer.**

_____

_____

_____

**Someone who ignored the rejection and
insults of others to pursue their godly desire.**

_____

_____

_____

**Someone whose specific request was not
fulfilled because God had a better answer.**

_____

_____

_____

9

REAL PEOPLE, REAL FAITH

Now faith is the assurance of things hoped for, the conviction
of things not seen. For by it the men of old gained approval.
(Hebrews 11:1–2)

Faith is not a trinket on a shelf that we take out and dust off when we need it. Faith is more like a muscle that has to be exercised daily to keep it strong and supple. Do you have good faith days and bad faith days? You can stay strong and active in your faith, whether you need atoning faith, life-giving faith, persevering faith, delivering faith, or creative faith.

Maintaining active faith is not always easy, but Hebrews 11 proves it's possible. This chapter is a parade of the heroes of faith. They encourage us, not only by their faith, but also because we can see that God uses ordinary people like you and me. Some failed the Lord at times, others had blatant weaknesses in some area of their lives. Most of them made a lot of mistakes along the way. Still, God saw their faith in Him and accomplished tremendous things through them.

Paul's letter to the Hebrews was written especially to the Jews—people who, like many of us, had difficulty believing what they could not see. Hebrews 11 reviews the faith of great men in Jewish history to demonstrate to Jewish believers in Christ that the faith God required of them was nothing new. It was the same faith that had motivated the Jewish race from its beginning.

This chapter wonderfully illustrates the diverse purposes and functions of faith. As you read these testimonies, consider the wonder and power of faith.

Atonement: Your Way or His Way?

Abel, the first man of faith listed in Hebrews 11, was looking for atonement. We all need forgiveness. Even though we know that Jesus has washed away all our sins, we need to go to Him, acknowledge our weaknesses, confess our sin, and claim our forgiveness.

The Jews, and all those who lived before Christ, offered sacrifices on the altar to obtain forgiveness. The very first sacrifices recorded in the Bible were those of Cain and Abel. Abel's was accepted, but Cain's was rejected (see Genesis 4:3–5).

Abel recognized that he was sinful and understood that the true way of atonement was to offer a blood sacrifice. Abel did not invent his own path to forgiveness; he did it God's way, demonstrating that he had no righteousness of his own. Abel knew that without the shedding of blood there is no remission of sin and threw himself on the mercy of God and was cleansed.

Cain, on the other hand, was probably singing that famous old song, *"I Did It My Way,"* as he came to the altar with the fruit of his hands. Cain was giving a thank offering, but there was no recognition of his sin or of his need of atonement. Abel showed that the right kind of faith does it *God's way!* Both he and his brother knew that there is no remission of sin without the shedding of blood, but Cain did not put faith into action. Abel brought a blood sacrifice. Cain's sacrifice was from the earth and from his own efforts.

Faith obeys God's Word. When you say that you believe (have faith) that your sins are washed away, are you speaking out of pride?

FAITH...

is certain about things that it cannot see **(Hebrews 11:1).**

is honorable **(Hebrews 11:2).**

governs our perception of the universe **(Hebrews 11:3).**

wins acceptance and rewards from God **(Hebrews 11:4).**

Are you harboring the thought that those sins were washed away because you are better than other people? Do you try to wash away your sins by doing "good works," going to church more often, or outperforming your neighbors?

Beware of offering a Cain sacrifice! Your faith for atonement must recognize that only God can wash away your sins. You must sacrifice any pride and turn your sins over to God.

Cain made another mistake: he was religious, but he wasn't faithful. He wanted to offer a sacrifice, but a bloodless one. He went through the motions, but his heart wasn't in it. How often do you "go through the motions" of reading your Bible, attending church, reciting prayers? None of these actions can nourish you unless your heart is filled with faith.

> And without faith it is impossible to please Him for he who comes to God must believe that He is, and that He is a rewarder of those who seek Him. (Hebrews 11:6)

In faith, we must actively, constantly focus on God and His salvation. He is not as interested in our actions as He is in our hearts. Reach out to Him in faith, and His love will fill your heart and your life.

The Man Who Never Died

The next man of faith mentioned in Hebrews 11 is Enoch, the man who never died. In the genealogy listed in Genesis 5, eight times we read: *"and he died,"* but in verses 21–24 we have a notable exception:

Enoch lived sixty-five years, and became the father of Methuselah. Then Enoch walked with God three hundred years after he became the father of Methuselah, and he had other sons and daughters. So all the days of Enoch were three hundred and sixty-five years. Enoch walked with God; and he was not, for God took him. (Genesis 5:21–24)

Enoch, the seventh generation from Adam, was taken up to heaven without seeing death. Less than 100 words are recorded about him, yet they are powerful words. Enoch was one of two men who the Bible says, *"walked with God."* There is no fault recorded about him. He is the only one, outside of Jesus, of whom it is written, *"he was pleasing to God"* (Hebrews 11:15); and he is one of only two who missed death! The days of Enoch were flagrantly wicked, but he preached righteousness and prophesied. Christ's second coming.

It was also about these men that Enoch, in the seventh generation from Adam, prophesied, saying, "Behold, the Lord came with many thousands of His holy ones, to execute judgment upon all, and to convict all the ungodly of all their ungodly deeds which they have done in an ungodly way, and of all the harsh things which ungodly sinners have spoken against Him." (Jude 1:14–15)

While others were just living, Enoch walked with God. His walk shows that he agreed with God, because *"Can two walk together, except they be agreed?"* (Amos 3:3 NKJV). Enoch pleased

God through his faith, for "... *without faith it is impossible to please Him...*" (Hebrews 11:6).

Enoch walked with God for 300 years. He didn't start walking with God until he was 65, after the birth of his first son, *Methuselah*. Methuselah's name means, "when he is dead it shall be sent." The "it" that would be sent refers to the flood. Methuselah lived the longest of all men, because God, in His great mercy, did not want to send the flood. The year Methuselah died the flood came.

Growing faith takes you into growing steps of blessing. Enoch went from faith to faith. After 300 years of daily walking in faith with God, he reached the apex of this faith—translation. He never tasted death! Enoch enjoyed a continuous fellowship with God. Nothing, not even death, interrupted that friendship. This pleasing walk of faith is available to you, too!

Enoch's Story!

Enoch actually had much in common with Elijah:

- Both were taken to heaven without dying.
- Both were prophets of judgment.
- Both fought against the ungodly.

Many believe that these two are the witnesses mentioned in Revelation 11, who will come to Earth to complete their lives and die.

The Faith that Saved the Human Race

The next Old Testament hero, Noah, also lived in a wicked generation and found grace in the eyes of the Lord.

By faith Noah, being warned by God about things not yet seen, in reverence prepared an ark for the salvation of his household, by which he condemned the world, and became an heir of the righteousness which is according to faith. (Hebrews 11:7)

The foundation of Noah's faith was God's Word—*"being warned by God."* He took God's Word as truth, even though he had no physical proof that the flood was actually going to happen; he believed *"things not yet seen."* Can you imagine building a huge boat in your backyard? What would the neighbors say? Maybe the newspapers and TV stations would come over to do a report on this crazy person! Perhaps your best friend would try to get you to see a psychiatrist! Noah's faith had to be really strong to withstand the ridicule that came from all sides.

Noah's faith was based on the Word of God and stayed strong in spite of what his eyes and ears told him. His faith led him to action: he *"prepared an ark"* and his action served as a witness to his faith *"by which he condemned the world"* (Hebrews 11:7). Best of all, that faith was rewarded in three wondrous ways: his family was saved, he became an heir of righteousness, and he was given a visible sign of God's faithfulness—the rainbow (see Genesis 6–9).

Noah acted on the Word of an invisible God, doing what seemed foolish to the casual bystander. He built an enormous boat and filled it with animals. He did what God said. He believed that God was telling him the truth when He warned of a great flood of judgment coming upon the earth. Noah had no visible signs of the flood until after he was locked inside the ark. For at least one hundred years, Noah built the ark to the exact specifications of his Lord. His faith delivered him and his entire family from being destroyed with the rest of mankind.

Can *your* faith overcome the ridicule of the world and deliver those you love from destruction? Yes, it can! I know, because I saw it happen in my own family. Shortly after I was married, my father had a nervous breakdown. My mother accompanied my husband and me to Dallas for a healing convention. One night, the evangelist called my mother out of the thousands of people present. He said, "You are weeping not for yourself, but for your husband, who has had a nervous breakdown. Take the handkerchief in which you have shed your tears, place it on his body, and he will be healed."

Some people might have said, "What can a used handkerchief do for a man who's had a nervous breakdown?" Surely this was as foolish as building an ark in the middle of a desert! My mother wasn't about to let thoughts like that get in her way! In faith, she took the handkerchief and followed the Lord's instructions. My father began to recover, not overnight, but day by day he improved.

Our heavenly Father has promised us that we will always have His loving kindness and mercy. When we became born-again believers, we became vessels to extend God's mercy and love to others—including our loved ones. We must reach forth, in faith, to touch and minister to those we love. With our hearts securely grounded in faith, we will know how to meet the needs of others.

Acting on the Word of God delivers us from His judgment! No

matter what is happening to the world around you, or what will happen, God is able to provide a way of escape, a place of safety! Have faith in God!

Eyes on the Eternal

Another hero who put his faith into action was Abraham. He was first called *Abram,* which means "exalted father." *Abraham,* which means "father of a multitude," was a man who followed God obediently without knowing where he was going. Abraham trusted God. He answered God's call on his life, followed His directions to a new land, always ready to move when God called. His eyes were not on his earthly inheritance, which was enormous, but on heavenly things. He was looking toward his permanent dwelling place. Abraham reveals that living in the elevated place of God's Word brings a *multitude* of results.

Abraham's wife Sarah had faith, too. God promised that she would be the *"mother of nations"* (see Genesis 17:16), but it looked to the world as if that promise would never be fulfilled. She was well past menopause and was childless. Abraham was no spring chicken, either, but they deeply desired to have a child.

What kind of faith would it take to believe God would provide a baby in their circumstances? Through her faith, Sarah received miracle-working power that quickened her body and Abraham's. This ninety-year-old woman gave birth to a child who would become a patriarch of Israel. In faith, Sarah kept her eyes on God and trusted in His promises.

Several years ago, a couple came to me in despair. Doctors had told them they could not have a child. I went out with them for coffee after a service one night, and I shared how God had miraculously given us a natural child. Doctors had told me the same thing: "You can never have a child." This couple said, "Would you agree in prayer for us?" So, we agreed in prayer, right there in the coffee shop. They moved away shortly after that, and I lost track of them for a while. Imagine my joy when they dropped by to show me a beautiful baby boy! Through faith, we receive healing and life!

Terrible Tragedy or Stunning Victory?

Following God in faith can be hard. Our faith can be tested in many ways at many times, but Abraham faced one of the most terrible tests of all and he passed with flying colors! He won the gold medal of faith. God asked him to sacrifice his and Sarah's only son, Isaac. Abraham had such faith in God's Word that he quietly did what God required, not understanding why, but knowing that—somehow—God would raise Isaac from the dead. By his actions, he proved his faith and trust in God and earned his title, "*father of faith*" (Genesis 22:1–18).

When you receive difficult commands from the Lord, it is a blessing to obey even when you don't understand the "why" of the instruction. Many of God's greatest blessings are lost when we say, "No," to the Lord because we are unwilling to take a risk. Abraham was willing to give up one son, and his descendants became as the sands of the sea. He was given back his son and countless more descendants. Your obedience to God brings a sure return every time!

Active Faith and Parenting

Imagine being a slave, expecting a child, and Pharaoh has ordered all newborns to be killed. When your baby is born, he is the most beautiful little boy! Wouldn't you be terrified of Pharaoh's decree?

Moses's parents actually had this experience. Amram and Jochebed were not afraid, because they had faith.

> *By faith Moses, when he was born, was hidden for three months by his parents, because they saw he was a beautiful child; and they were not afraid of the king's edict.*
> (Hebrews 11:23)

To have this kind of faith, Amram and Jochebed must have heard from God, because faith can come only from hearing the Word of God. *Amram* means "a people exalted." His son was to be part of a divine plan that would exalt his people. *Jochebed* means "Jehovah is glory." She glorified God with her active faith. These parents saw only slavery and evil coming from their earthly ruler, but they looked beyond that to God, and knew that He was in control.

Amram and Jochebed's faith gave them the strength to put their tiny baby into a basket and float him down the river. They knew in their hearts that God had a plan and turned their baby over to God's care. As parents, we can fret and worry over our children, or we can turn them over to God, Who loves them even more than we do.

Faith Makes Hard Choices

There is more about Moses than any other individual in the eleventh chapter of Hebrews. His life was marked by crises. He was the child of slaves in Egypt. To rescue him from Pharaoh's plan to kill all male babies, his parents placed him in a basket and sent him down the Nile River.

The daughter of Pharaoh rescued him and raised him as her own son. He became a leader. How interesting that the Pharaoh who desired to keep Israel permanently enslaved, would give food, lodging, and education to the very man who would bring about Israel's freedom (see Exodus 2:1–10)!

In spite of all the earthly privileges in Pharaoh's house, Moses refused to be called the son of Pharaoh's daughter. Instead, he chose to identify with his own people. He knew that God had called him to deliver his people from slavery, and he would rather be a godly slave than a heathen king. He would rather suffer with the people of God than enjoy the pleasures of sin. He knew all about the pleasures that were available to him at the palace—perhaps even a future as Pharaoh—but he resolutely refused them!

> **Faith can only come by hearing the Word of God.**

Moses had a revelation of the coming Messiah. He knew that suffering with Him, whatever the cost, was a greater treasure than all the riches of Egypt. In Christ there are true treasures that cannot be compared with any glitter the world might offer.

Moses knew that if he obeyed the voice of God, there would be a reward. This reward was unseen. Respect God's reward; it will help you to live the faith life diligently. Look to Him, not men.

That will keep your faith alive and not disappointed! Keep your eyes on God's goals.

Faith Crosses the Waters

Moses would eventually lead the Hebrews out of Egypt. They were leaving a place of slavery and poverty, just as we escaped the slavery and poverty of Satan's world when we accepted Jesus as our Savior.

Like us, the Israelites were under a new Lord, but the old one didn't give up easily. Pharaoh fought long and hard to keep the Israelites, but he finally let them go. He was angry because they left, angry about the many deaths in Egypt, and angry that he had lost free labor. He was determined to bring them back.

Satan seldom gives up his slaves of sin without a fight. Moses encouraged the people to move on in faith, and God rewarded their faith. He opened the Red Sea, and they crossed over to safety from their enemies! They were in a hard place: the sea was before them, the army behind them—but they stepped out in faith (see Exodus 14:15–18).

God has creative ways to get us over seemingly impossible obstacles! Pharaoh was sure he had won. His former slaves were trapped between the Red Sea and the biggest army in the world. They would never get away! How could Pharaoh have imagined that big sea dividing to reveal a way of escape? Who could have imagined that Moses would have enough faith to stay calm in the face of sure destruction, and reach out his arm in faith?

God can use our faith to open paths where every way seems closed off. Once God told me to pass out Bibles to Jewish people, but I soon discovered that Israeli law forbids Bibles to be passed out in that country. Still, my faith was strong that God wanted me to proceed with this plan. God is so creative in overcoming obstacles. At that time, 30,000 Jewish soldiers were stationed in Lebanon. The Lord told me, "Cross the border. Lebanon has no such laws." We crossed the border and passed out Bibles to all those soldiers! It was such a blessing to watch young men sitting on tanks and reading the New Testament.

When you face obstacles so big that you see no way around them, just remember that God has prepared a miracle. Reach out in faith, and He will carry you across "... *and nothing will be impossible to you*" (Matthew 17:20).

When you accept the salvation of Jesus, you anger Satan! Just like Pharaoh, Satan is angry that you have left his sinful traps behind and angry that he has lost control of your behavior. He will come after you, and push you to your limits, hoping to capture you.

When this happens, remember Moses and the Israelites! If you are trapped between Satan's army and the Red Sea, step out in faith. Your faith will be unfailingly rewarded. The Lord is just as much your deliverer as He was Moses's deliverer!

You Can Be a Faith Hero, Too!

Your faith and walk with God can please Him. He wants to have continuous, unbroken fellowship with His children. Like Enoch, you can agree with God, and spend your lifetime walking in harmony with Him. Doing things God's way, even when we don't understand it, will always bring a blessing.

Faith delivered Noah and his whole household during an age when the rest of the world was in rebellion against God. Noah survived ridicule and, through faith, overcame doubt. He trusted God's Word even when his eyes and ears gave him different messages. His reward was the saving of his family from destruction and an everlasting promise from God.

Abraham was called to walk away from his actual family to become the patriarch of an intangible one. In faith, he followed God's voice, and was rewarded with riches in this life. Abraham

Works of Faith

In Hebrews 11:33–38, we are reminded of the "works" of the Old Testament faith heroes. Their stories show what *your* active faith can accomplish:

- Subdue kingdoms (Joshua 12:1–24)
- Produce righteousness (Genesis 15:6)
- Obtain promises (Genesis 21:1–3)
- Strengthen believers (Judges 7:12–15)
- Put armies to flight (1 Samuel 17:51-52)
- Endure torture (Genesis 39:20)
- Resist temptation (Genesis 39:1–17)
- Withstand wandering and afflictions (2 Kings 17–18)

proved his faith and trust in God when he dared to obey God and offered his son as a sacrifice. He learned during his faith walk that God is true to His Word.

Moses's parents were full of faith to believe that God had a future for their son who was condemned by Pharaoh to die. No matter how hopeless it may seem for your son or daughter, have faith that God can redeem your present circumstances and turn them around for a blessing. Moses learned to know God step by step as he followed Him in obedience. He did not have the written Word as we do; he had to listen daily to God's voice and be obedient. That was the greatest qualification for an effective leader in those days, and it still is today:

"So faith comes from hearing, and hearing by the word of Christ." (Romans 10:17)

Studying this list of men and women, you can see that God gives faith for every situation in every age. He is your source of faith. God's kind of faith covers every circumstance you will ever face.

God will never call you to a place or a work without equipping you fully to be successful. Some received faith to do the impossible, others to endure ridicule, and some to give up earthly pleasures— but they were all rewarded for their faith! God will meet you where you are with His kind of faith. Receive His faith and be a vessel for His use. Faith can only increase as it is used. So put your faith into action!

Sometimes Faith Stands Still

When the Israelites saw Pharaoh's armies coming toward them from the west, and the Red Sea facing them in the east, they began to cry out to the Lord and to complain to Moses. Moses's response was, *"Do not fear! Stand by, and see the salvation of the Lord"* (Exodus 14:13). More than 330 times in the Bible, we find the expression *"Fear not."* God is constantly calming our fears.

When you are worried or afraid, do you start running around trying to fix things? Active faith is not always doing things! Sometimes God just wants you to be quiet.

Here is what can happen when we stand still:

- Stand still, and see the salvation of the Lord (Exodus 14:13; 2 Chronicles 20:17).
- Stand still, that you may hear (Numbers 9:8).
- Stand still, and consider the wondrous works of God (Job 37:14).

STEPS TO BELIEVING BIG

1.

Record two events where your faith
delivered you from Satan's trap.

_____

_____

_____

2.

You can be a leader like Moses.
Each one of us is a leader in some capacity.
You may be the leader at your job, in your
neighborhood, at your church or in your family.

Study the leadership qualities discussed in
1 Timothy chapters 3 and 4. List as many as
you can. Then pray and ask God to develop you
in the leadership area that He has for you.

_____

_____

_____

_____

3.

Find and meditate on a scripture for each
of these kinds of faith:

Atoning Faith _____

Life-giving Faith _____

Persevering Faith _____

Delivering Faith _____

Creative Faith _____

4.

Has God ever asked you to do a difficult thing?
Share your situation and response
with a friend or mentor today.

5.

Meditate on Matthew 17:10. How will
this help you put feet to your faith?
Record your thoughts here.

_____
_____
_____
_____

10

YOU HAVE FRIENDS
IN HIGH PLACES

*Therefore as you have received Christ Jesus the Lord, so walk in
Him, having been firmly rooted and now being built up in Him
and established in your faith, just as you were instructed, and
overflowing with gratitude.* (Colossians 2:6–7)

Have you ever been lonely or just needed someone to talk to,
someone who understands you and accepts you just the way
you are?

You may know that God is Savior, King, and the source of all
blessings, but did you know that He also wants to be your friend?
It's true! God wants to spend time with you. He wants to walk
with you and hear about your troubles, your trying times, and
your happy moments. He wants to talk with you *all* the time. He

wants to fellowship with you on *every* level. You need never be lonely with a friend like Him!

The Lord calls us into fellowship with Him. We usually feel as though we are calling upon Him, but God loves conversing with us.

One morning, I was praying at our kitchen table and telling the Lord what a privilege it is to live for Him. He spoke to me and said, "You don't live *for me*, you live *with me*. We live together, and we are seated together in heavenly places. We meet together in daily fellowship when we join in prayer." Isn't it wonderful! We are never alone, because He is *Jehovah-Shammah*—"The Lord is There." God said in Hebrews 13:5, *"I will never leave you nor forsake you"* (MEV). Why? Because He has called us into constant fellowship.

You're in Good Company

If you take a walk with your Best Friend every day (just the two of you), you will find your faith growing and your blessings multiplying. The Bible is a how-to manual on walking with God. Let's look at four of the great people in the Bible who walked with God: Enoch, Noah, Moses, and Paul.

Enoch was the first person whom the Bible says *"walked with God"* (Genesis 5:22). He had fellowship with God on such an intimate level that God recorded the experience. Enoch put friendship and fellowship with God above all other things.

Some years later, a descendant of Enoch's, Noah, did the same. He walked with God in spite of the fact that his whole generation was going in another direction. Noah maintained fellowship with God to such an extent that God shared His plans with him. God told him how disappointed He was in man and how He planned to destroy all mankind with a flood.

Noah trusted God's Word. His fellowship with God had taught him to listen to God. God told Noah how to save all his household from destruction and Noah did not hesitate to obey. His fellowship with God had built faith in him. He believed God unreservedly, because he was walking and talking with God. His reward was life for himself and his family.

Walking With God

Enoch and Noah are the only people who the Bible says, *"walked with God."* The word for "walk" is the Hebrew word *halak*, which means "to walk up and down, to be conversant." Later, Moses is said to have walked and talked with God, in much the same way that Adam did.

An Honest Relationship

Another man in the Bible who desired to know God was Moses. He knew the name of God. The Lord spoke to Moses face to face, just as a man speaks to his friend. I love the relationship that Moses had with God. He revered God, worshiped Him, loved Him—and got upset with Him from time to time!

When God first called Moses to lead His people out of Egypt, Moses didn't want the job. He said, *"Lord, please! Send someone else*" (Exodus 4:13 TLB). Moses's reluctance angered God, but He listened and appointed Aaron to be Moses's spokesperson. Here, two good friends get annoyed with each other, but continue to love and serve each other!

When Moses first asked Pharaoh to let the Israelites go, Pharaoh responded by increasing the slaves' workload. Moses went to God and said,

> *"O Lord, why have You brought trouble on this people? Why is it You have sent me?"* (Exodus 5:22 NKJV)

God's response to Moses was beautiful. He comforted Moses by reminding him of the promises that He made to the Israelites. He encouraged Moses by repeating the promise to bring the people to the promised land.

So often, when we think we are doing God's will, things turn out differently from what we expect. That's the time to go back to God and tell Him how you feel. Ask Him why things aren't working out the way you expected. Let Him encourage and comfort you.

Moses had a deep desire to know and understand God. When we care about someone, we want to know everything there is to know about them. That's how Moses felt about God. He said to the Lord,

> *"... Let me know Your ways that I may know You, so that I may find favor in Your sight."* (Exodus 33:13)

If we want a deep friendship with God, we need to get to know Him.

As Moses led the people through dangers and hardships, many times he lost his patience with their complaints and bickering. God sent manna to the people daily, yet they grumbled because they were bored with the same food every day. There is a wonderful conversation between God and Moses in Numbers 11:10–15. They were both getting tired of these people who were never satisfied. Moses was upset, and he let God know exactly how he felt. Moses said to God:

> *"Why have You been so hard on Your servant? And why have I not found favor in Your sight, that You have laid the burden of all this people on me? Was it I who conceived all this people? Was it I who brought them forth . . . ? Where am I to get meat to give to all this people? For they weep before me, saying, 'Give us meat that we may eat!' I alone am not able to carry all this people, because it is too burdensome for me. So if You are going to deal thus with me, please kill me at once . . ."* (Numbers 11:11–15)

God's response is wonderful. He appoints 70 elders to assist Moses and to lift his burden. God says to Moses:

> *"They shall bear the burden of the people with you, so that you will not bear it all alone."* (Numbers 11:17)

Isn't it fantastic to know that God understands our burdens? Sometimes we think we have to manage everything on our own. When God gives us a task to do, we try to come up with the energy, patience, and wisdom to follow through on our own.

How much better to just be honest with God, to tell Him that we are tired or frustrated. God hears us when we speak to Him as a trusted friend and tell Him exactly how we feel. He does not expect us to carry the burdens of this life alone. Go to Him in faith and tell him exactly how you feel. Get into fellowship with Him, and He will lighten your burdens.

Advising God

A little later, Moses was able to comfort God! When it was time to go up into the promised land, the people were afraid of the armies they would be facing. Fearful, they wanted to go back to Egypt. This infuriated God, and He said to Moses:

"How long will this people spurn Me? And how long will they not believe in Me, despite all the signs which I have performed in their midst? I will smite them with pestilence and dispossess them, and I will make you into a nation greater and mightier than they." (Numbers 14:11–12)

God was furious with His people and ready to destroy them, but Moses had some "advice" for God. He reminded God that His reputation was at stake and that if God destroyed these people whom He had just led out of slavery,

"Then the Egyptians will hear of it, for by Your strength You brought up this people from their midst, and they will tell it

to the inhabitants of this land. They have heard that You, O
Lord, are in the midst of this people, for You, O Lord, are
seen eye to eye, while Your cloud stands over them; and You go
before them in a pillar of cloud by day and in a pillar of fire by
night. Now if You slay this people as one man, then the nations
who have heard of Your fame will say, 'Because the Lord could
not bring this people into the land which He promised them by
oath." (Numbers 14:13–16)

Have you ever given advice to God? It's a strange thing to think
that God might want our advice. He doesn't need us to tell Him what
to do, but He does want our friendship, and a friend is always honest.

He also wants us to listen to Him and to understand His ways.
Because Moses had walked so intimately for so long with God, he
knew God's plans and methods. As a result, Moses's advice to
God was absolutely in line with God's design. Moses was actually
quoting God's own words back to Him. Look at the rest of Moses's
advice to God:

"'The Lord is slow to anger and abundant in loving kindness,
forgiving iniquity and transgression; but He will by no means
clear the guilty, visiting the iniquity of the fathers on the
children to the third and the fourth generations.' Pardon, I
pray, the iniquity of this people according to the greatness
of Your loving kindness, just as You also have forgiven this
people, from Egypt even until now." (Numbers 14:18–19)

Moses was simply reminding God of the promises that He had
made and of the words that He had spoken. God must have been

delighted that Moses knew Him so well!

What was the result of this advice of Moses? God forgave the people! How does a humble man give advice to God, and have his advice followed? Let's look at the components of this amazing conversation.

Friends First

Moses established a relationship with God. He talked to God, followed God's commands, and was faithful to Him. If you walk up to a complete stranger and offer your advice, is it likely to be accepted? It takes a long and faithful friendship to be able to give and take advice.

Next, Moses dedicated himself to God's plan. Remember, God offered to destroy the Israelites and raise up another nation made up of Moses's descendants. What glory that would have given to Moses! However, Moses knew that this was not in God's perfect plan. Moses's advice to God was designed to bring glory to God, not to Moses.

Moses based his advice on God's own words and promises. He didn't make a plan of his own. He listened to God, and stored God's Word in his heart. He had faith that every one of God's promises would be kept.

Have you ever tried to tell God what to do? Have you said, "Now, God, You need to do this miracle for me"? If you are going to tell God what to do, you need to follow Moses's example. Spend time with God, become His friend, store up His Word in your heart, and dedicate yourself to His glory, not your own. All these things will strengthen your faith and relationship with God, so that when you come to Him with your prayers, they will be in line with His desires. When these things are in place, prayers get answered!

A Simple Goal

In the New Testament, Paul was a man who walked with God. We know that Paul established and encouraged many of the early churches, and that he wrote divinely inspired letters which continue to guide believers today. If you had asked Paul what his life's work was, he would not have said "building churches" or "writing epistles." Paul's life's work—the greatest longing of his heart—was simply to fellowship with Christ.

> *I count all things to be loss in view of the surpassing value of knowing Christ Jesus my Lord, for whom I have suffered the loss of all things, and count them but rubbish so that I may gain Christ, and may be found in Him.*
> (Philippians 3:8–9)

Paul dedicated himself to knowing God. That was his first priority. The result was a deep and unshakable faith that was so glorious, Paul was compelled to share it with others. *Out of fellowship came faith and out of faith came a ministry which changed the world.*

Fellowship with God is a lifelong project. Everything else must be subordinate to it. It is too easy to slip into the "works" mode and forget the relationship. If your fellowship time with God leads you to volunteer at your church or to testify to unbelievers, then you have your priorities straight. Be vigilant that your good works don't take up so much time and energy that you neglect your personal relationship with God.

I really enjoyed teaching Bible school students who were serious and committed—hungry and purposed to know God's Word and His Son Jesus in a personal way. However, through the years I have watched people backslide while in Bible school, and I have wondered, "How can that happen when they receive in-depth Bible teaching *daily*?"

After questioning some of them, and through prayer, I have discovered that Bible students, as strange as it seems, often neglected their own personal daily relationship with the Lord. They mistakenly thought their classes took the place of personal time with God.

What a dangerous mistake! Each one of us, no matter what our call, must have a close, daily relationship with our loving heavenly Father. When we are overburdened with things of the world—work, family, problems, relationships, financial difficulties—we tend to "shelve" the reading of the Word. It may make worldly sense to put God "on hold," but it never makes sense spiritually.

Who Wants to Be *My* Friend?

When we are down on ourselves and feeling like failures, it's hard to imagine anyone wanting to be our friend. It is harder to imagine that a perfect God, the King of Kings, Lord of Lords, wants our friendship. Yet, the Bible tells us that God is the one who is reaching out to us. He chooses to dwell in us and fellowship with us.

God said to the Israelites, *"I will dwell among the sons of Israel and will be their God"* (Exodus 29:45). After the Babylonian captivity, during the restoration of the temple, God gave us another assurance of His desire to dwell among us:

> *"Sing for joy and be glad, O daughter of Zion; for behold I am coming and I will dwell in your midst,"* declares the LORD. (Zechariah 2:10)

Jesus relates to us on an even more intimate level: He calls us to be His friends!

> *"You are My friends if you do what I command you. No longer do I call you slaves, for the slave does not know what his master is doing; but I have called you friends, for all things that I have heard from My Father I have made known to you. You did not choose Me but I chose you, and appointed you, that you should go and bear fruit, and that your fruit should remain, so that whatever you ask of the Father in My name He may give to you."* (John 15:14–16)

Do you remember how it felt when you wished and hoped that the "popular" kids in school would choose you as a friend? Look again at the scripture above. The coolest person of all has chosen you for His friend.

What A Friend!

How much does God want your friendship? Again and again in the Bible, God made a way for fallen man to return to Him. He provided a sacrifice for Adam and Eve, made a covenant with Abraham, gave the law to Israel, and finally, *"God so loved the world that He gave His only begotten Son"* (John 3:16).

Why did God send Jesus? *"God is faithful, through whom you were called into fellowship with His Son, Jesus Christ our Lord"* (1 Corinthians 1:9). God desires your fellowship so much that He even gave His only son to restore your relationship with Him.

What's the Catch?

Have you ever had a friend who took advantage of you? Perhaps money was borrowed and never repaid. Maybe your friend moved in with you, ate your food, messed up your house, and never lifted a hand to help or repay you. Worse, your friend may have gossiped about you behind your back. That hurts! What did you do?

You can still love and pray for a friend like that, but you don't have to continue to spend time with someone who abuses you. Healthy people set sensible boundaries on their relationships.

God, in His infinite wisdom, established standards of friendship. He wants your fellowship, but there are conditions.

Obey the Law

God did not give us the Ten Commandments to make Himself feel powerful and important! Those laws were established for our own good. He gave us His statutes out of love and concern for us. Would a good friend ignore or reject such a gift?

One of the conditions of friendship with God is obedience to His laws.

> *"If you walk in My statutes and keep My commandments . . . I will also walk among you and be your God, and you shall be My people."* (Leviticus 26:3, 12)

Turn on the Light

The second condition of fellowship is to "walk in the Light." Walk where He is, where His Word leads you! Jesus is the Light of the World. We are to walk in that Light. If we continue to walk in darkness, we do not have fellowship with God or one another.

> *And this is the message we have heard from Him and announce to you, that God is Light, and in Him there is no darkness at all. If we say that we have fellowship with Him and yet walk in the darkness, we lie and do not practice the truth; but if we walk in the Light as He Himself is in the Light, we have fellowship with one another, and the blood of Jesus His Son cleanses us from all sin.* (1 John 1:5–7)

Your walk with God will produce powerful results. As your fellowship deepens, so will your faith. As your faith grows, so will your desire for fellowship. Being friends with God is such a wonderful experience that we could be satisfied with that alone, but our God is a God of abundance. Fellowship with God brings many other blessings.

The Heavens Will Open

As you grow closer to God, you will be filled with the desire to obey Him. God does not want blind obedience—He wants love and fellowship. Obedience is a sign of your love and fellowship.

> "Now, Israel, what does the LORD your God require from you, but to fear the LORD your God, to walk in all His ways and love Him, and to serve the LORD your God with all your heart and with all your soul, and to keep the LORD's commandments and His statutes which I am commanding you today for your good?" (Deuteronomy 10:12–13)

When you become obedient, physical and material prosperity follows. Some of the blessings promised to the obedient are listed in Deuteronomy 28:1–6, and they are fabulous:

> "Now it shall be, if you will diligently obey the LORD your God, being careful to do all His commandments which I command you today, the LORD your God will set you high above all the nations of the earth. All these blessings will come upon you and overtake you, if you will obey the LORD your God:

"Blessed shall you be in the city, and blessed shall you be in the country.

"Blessed shall be the offspring of your body and the produce of your ground and the offspring of your beasts, the increase of your herd and the young of your flock.

"Blessed shall be your basket and your kneading bowl.

"Blessed shall you be when you come in, and blessed shall you be when you go out."

You Will Bear Fruit

As you continue to fellowship with God and actualize His abiding in your life, you will bear fruit. In other words, as the presence of Christ in your life becomes more and more real to you, it affects everything you do: your efforts are fruitful; you accomplish what you set out to do; you have the energy to fulfill what God wants of you. Learn to let Jesus live His life through you!

"Abide in Me, and I in you. As the branch cannot bear fruit of itself unless it abides in the vine, so neither can you unless you abide in Me. I am the vine, you are the branches; he who abides in Me, and I in him, he bears much fruit, for apart from Me you can do nothing." (John 15:4–5)

This verse reminds me of Freda Lindsay, who was president of Christ for the Nations. At a very young age, Freda found the Lord.

She was never a yo-yo Christian—up one day and down the next. From the time she met the Lord, she literally grafted herself onto the living vine! She stuck to His Word. She was in constant fellowship with Him. In fact, she once told me that she had read through her Bible 52 times!

When Freda's husband Gordon passed away, she took on the awesome responsibility of directing the school's ministry, even though she felt incapable of the task. God alone gave her the wisdom to successfully guide this international organization.

As Freda shared this information with me, I thought, "So many times, we bear the fruit of who we are." Christ for the Nations is a school where both young and old men and women come forth in the same power of God's Word and Spirit. Like Freda, these people learn to fellowship with the Lord, follow Him, and love Him with all their hearts.

Prayers Will Be Answered

Your power in prayer is directly related to your fellowship with God. It is not a "you be good, and I will reward you" syndrome. It is a life principle throughout the Word. Our walk, communion, and knowledge of God produce the power for answered prayer.

"If you abide in Me, and My words abide in you, ask whatever you wish, and it will be done for you." (John 15:7)

As we come to know God better, we begin to understand His ways—the method He would choose to solve a problem. The more we know Him, the more God-like our prayers become. When our prayers are in line with His will, there is no doubt that they will be answered.

More Promises...

Deuteronomy 28:7–14 adds these promises:

- Your enemies will be defeated and flee from you.
- The Lord will bless everything you put your hand to.
- The world will see that you are the Lord's and will fear you. He will give you abundant prosperity.
- He will open the heavens, the storehouse of His bounty.
- You will lend to many, but borrow from none.
- You will always be at the top, not the bottom.

Believers Will Be United

As our fellowship with God brings us into line with His thinking, it also brings us into unity with others in the body of Christ. We all have the mind of Christ as believers, yet it is constant fellowship with Him that teaches us how to express His mind in our daily lives.

As each member of His body expresses God's thoughts, clashes between us are diminished. This unity of believers is Christ's desire, for this is how His bride, the church, prepares for His coming. Jesus prayed just before Judas's betrayal:

"I pray also for those who will believe in me through their message, that all of them may be one, Father, just as you are in me and I am in you. May they also be in us so that the world may believe that you have sent me. I have given them the glory that you gave me, that they may be one as we are one—I in them and you in me—so that they may be brought to complete unity. Then the world will know that you sent me and have loved them even as you have loved me." (John 17:20–23 NIV)

Unity among believers is a sign to the world that Christ is the Son of God. When believers quarrel, become divided, and take sides against each other, it is a sure sign that we are not walking in fellowship with God. When we devote our time and energy to our friendship with Him, we become unified with other believers who are also walking with Him. *"The one who says he abides in Him ought himself to walk in the same manner as He walked"* (1 John 2:6). When we are all walking in the same direction—His direction—the world sees the wonder of God's love!

Fellowship—Right

The Bible tells us to establish fellowship with:

- God the Father (Deuteronomy 6:5, 10:12, 11:1; Matthew 22:37–38; 1 John 4:8–19)
- God the Son (2 Peter 3:18; 1 John 5:1–4; John 14:23–24)
- God the Holy Spirit (John 14:26, 16:13–15; Ephesians 4:30; Romans 8:1–16; 2 Corinthians 3:17–18; Galatians 4:6, 5:16–26, 6:8)
- Other believers (John 13:34–35; Ephesians 4:1–6; 1 Thessalonians 4:9; 1 John 4:20–21)

Fellowship—Wrong

**The Bible speaks of many with whom
we are not to have fellowship:**

- The ungodly (Psalm 1:1)
- Scorners (Psalm 1:1)
- Workers of iniquity (Psalm 6:8)
- Deceitful persons (Psalm 26:4)
- Evildoers (Psalm 26:5)
- Criminals (Proverbs 1:10–15)
- The foolish (Proverbs 14:7)
- The angry man (Proverbs 22:24)
- Excommunicated church member (Matthew 18:17)
- Those causing divisions (Romans 16:17 NKJV)
- Backsliders (2 John 9)
- False Teachers (1 Timothy 6:3–5; 2 John 10)
- The disorderly (2 Timothy 3:6)
- The disobedient (2 Timothy 3:13)
- Unbelievers (2 Corinthians 6:14)
- Fornicators, idolaters, drunkards, and swindlers
  (1 Corinthians 5:9–11)
- Self-lovers, boasters, the proud, the ungrateful
  (2 Timothy 3:2)
- The unforgiving, slanderous, brutal (2 Timothy 3:3)
- The treacherous, conceited, and lovers of pleasure
  (2 Timothy 3:4)
- Hypocrites (2 Timothy 3:5)

UNITY AMONG BELIEVERS IS A SIGN TO THE WORLD THAT CHRIST IS THE SON OF GOD. WHEN BELIEVERS QUARREL, BECOME DIVIDED, AND TAKE SIDES AGAINST EACH OTHER, IT IS A SURE SIGN THAT WE ARE NOT WALKING IN FELLOWSHIP WITH GOD.

When Fellowship is Broken

Fellowship is a two-way conversation. God already knows all there is to know about you, but He wants your voluntary communication. If you have sinned (as we all do every day, in some way) you must confess it to Him. He will wash away the guilt and instantly forget your sin—but first you must bring it to Him.

> *If we say that we have fellowship with Him and yet walk in the darkness, we lie and do not practice the truth.*
> (1 John 1:6)

If your sins are unconfessed, there is a wall between you and God. He does not hear you. You may pray with what you call faith, but your prayer gets you nowhere. Sin has stopped communication between you and your God.

> *"Behold, the LORD's hand is not so short that it cannot save; nor is His ear so dull that it cannot hear. But your iniquities have made a separation between you and your God, and your sins have hidden His face from you, so that He does not hear."*
> (Isaiah 59:1–2)

David sinned with Bathsheba. For many months he regarded this iniquity in his heart without repentance. Psalm 32:3–4 explains how he felt during this time:

> *When I kept silent, about my sin, my body wasted away through my groaning all day long. For day and night Your*

hand was heavy upon me; my vitality was drained away as
with the fever heat of summer. Selah.

David's fellowship with God had been broken. His prayers were
not answered, and he felt like a sick man.

If you are troubled with lack of answered prayer, make sure
there is no cause for broken fellowship with your Lord. The source
of our faith is God and His Word. If our fellowship with the source
is broken, the supply of faith is also affected. We know that the
source is within us, but He cannot work through us when sin is
in the way. Unconfessed sin stops faith from working in our lives.

Now for the good news. Your fellowship can be restored
instantly! God is always waiting with love and an open heart to
welcome you back.

When we sin, the devil loves to use it as a wedge to control our
lives. He would like us to spend our time going over every wrong
thing we ever did. He loves it when we send ourselves into a pit
of despair and self-pity.

Another technique that Satan uses is to get us so busy with our
affairs that we barely notice when we have sinned. Don't listen to
the voice of the liar. Listen instead to the voice of the Holy Spirit.
When you know you have sinned, don't cover it up with an excuse
or blame it on someone else. Call it what it is—sin.

Search me, O God, and know my heart; try me and know my
anxious thoughts; and see if there be any hurtful way in me, and
lead me in the everlasting way. (Psalm 139:23–24)

If you have, for instance, been lax in your prayer life, acknowledge your sin, and ask forgiveness. God says in 1 Thessalonians 5:17 for us to *"pray without ceasing."* If He has shown you that you have not been praying as He said, you cannot say to God, "But, you know how busy I have been." You can say, "I have been disobedient; I have put other things ahead of my fellowship with you. Forgive my sin."

Repentance involves both a turning *from* sin and a turning to God. It is not just a repetition of the things done—not just a verbal recitation of offenses—it is a life-changing process. The way back to fellowship is to accept your responsibility for sin, confess it to Him, and then trust Him to forgive it completely.

Live in Forgiveness

Each day you fellowship with God, it grows more precious. Your time with Him becomes the first priority in your life. You are walking in the light of His Word. He shows you treasures from His Word and reveals His plans for your life—He gives you a vision of the work He plans to do through you. It is the life of Christ that meets the needs of others through you. He is reaching out to you, asking you to walk in fellowship with Him. Accept His invitation. Be strong in your fellowship with God. It will make you strong in your faith in Him! Your life will never be the same!

STEPS TO BELIEVING BIG

1.

Tell God that you want and need His friendship.
Commit to talk with Him at least ten minutes every
day. As your fellowship grows, you will find yourself
wanting to spend more and more time with Him.

2.
List three ways you are walking in the Light and
three ways you are still walking in darkness.

Light_____

_____

_____

Darkness_____

_____

_____

3.

Read and meditate on Psalm 51. Mediate
on the steps David took in his prayer to the
Lord. Share these steps with a friend.

4.

Commit to reading through the Bible in a year. As you read daily, write down new revelations.

- What does God say He will do?
- What does God say you are to do?
- Who does God say He is?
- Who does God say you are?
- What is He like?
- What are His desires?
- What are His methods?
- What are His plans?

5.

Look up "forgiveness" in a concordance and write down at least five verses about this topic. Meditate on how you can put them into practice this week.

_____

_____

_____

_____

_____

_____

_____

11

GATEWAY TO PROSPERITY—FAITH

Beloved, I pray that in all respects you may prosper and be in good health, just as your soul prospers. (3 John 2)

God wants us to prosper financially and in everything. He doesn't want us to settle for "just enough." He wants to pour down so many blessings that your storehouse is overflowing!

Prosperity for His children is a theme throughout the Bible. From the very beginning, God gave Adam prosperity. In the garden of Eden, Adam could find everything he needed for abundant living. Later, God made a covenant with His chosen people, and prosperity was a big part of His promise to the Israelites.

The LORD will make you abound in prosperity, in the offspring of your body and in the offspring of your beast and in the

*produce of your ground, in the land which the LORD swore to
your fathers to give you.* (Deuteronomy 28:11)

God conferred upon the Israelites the power to acquire wealth
so that they would demonstrate to the world the power and generosity of their God, and His faithfulness in keeping promises.

*But you shall remember the LORD your God, for it is He who
is giving you power to make wealth, that He may confirm
His covenant which He swore to your fathers, as it is this day.*
(Deuteronomy 8:18)

Just as He did for the Israelites, God has also given you the
power to make wealth. God has already wrapped your gift! It is
not a stingy little gift; it's an unlimited treasure. God wants you
to rejoice over the blessings He sends you.

*Let them shout for joy and rejoice, who favor my vindication;
and let them say continually, "The LORD be magnified, who
delights in the prosperity of His servant."* (Psalm 35:27)

There will always be someone who wants to steal what you have.
Satan, the thief *"comes only to steal and kill and destroy"* (John
10:10). He steals your wealth by making you doubt that you deserve
it. He loves to discourage you and make you think, *Well, I'm just
supposed to be poor.*

How can you protect your prosperity from the thief? How can
you appropriate the prosperity that God wants to shower upon you?

To live in biblical prosperity, you must walk in the truth. He says, *"I have no greater joy than this, to hear of my children walking in the truth"* (3 John 4). Walking in truth will build your faith and cause you to prosper in every way.

God has given you the power to make wealth.

It is important to believe that God wants you to prosper. People sometimes say, "Well, Jesus is my example and He was poor, so I'm supposed to be poor." Be careful to understand the difference between Jesus as your example and Jesus as your substitute.

Jesus is our *example* as a servant. We are to serve others as He did. Jesus is our example in love and authority and dominion. We are to walk in His steps in all these things. However, Jesus acted as our substitute when He paid the price for our sins. We are not to take on the sins or sicknesses of others, because in this, Jesus was not setting an example; He was acting as a *substitute*.

Jesus is also our *substitute* in poverty. He did not live as a poor man to set an example for us. He became poor so that we might be rich. Prosperity is your covenant right.

Though He was rich, yet for your sake He became poor, so that you through His poverty might become rich.
(2 Corinthians 8:9)

To receive your blessings, you need to claim them. Make this confession: "God wishes above all things that I might prosper and be in good health, as my soul prospers."

Several years ago, a pastor in Niagara Falls told me of a time when his area desperately needed rain. Many of the men in his congregation were farmers and their situation had been growing steadily worse. Without rain, all the crops would be ruined. The pastor reminded his congregation that God didn't desire poverty and hard times to fall upon them; God wanted them to prosper. The congregation studied the promises in the Bible and began to pray and ask God to deliver the prosperity that He promised. The rain came and the crops were saved!

Your Hottest Investment Opportunity

Have you ever tried to save money? Maybe you put a $20 bill away in the back of a drawer. Several months later, when you went back to get that $20 bill, how much money was there? You still had exactly $20. Your treasure hadn't grown one bit. In fact, with inflation, it may have been worth even less than when you put it aside. Worse, someone may have stolen it out of the drawer, leaving you with nothing.

> *"Do not store up for yourselves treasures upon earth, where moth and rust destroy, and where thieves break in and steal. But store up for yourselves treasures in heaven, where neither moth nor rust destroys, and where thieves do not break in or steal; for where your treasure is, there your heart will be also."* (Matthew 6:19–21)

For your money to grow, it has to be invested. What you invest in God's kingdom will come back to you multiplied many times. Investments in God's kingdom return the very highest rate of all. Store up treasures in heaven; then, when you have a need, you can begin to draw from that account.

Seeing Money Through God's Eyes— Millionaire Faith for Your Finances

In God's economy, materialism and how the world values money can hurt you (see Proverbs 15:6). Real prosperity comes out of the prosperity of your soul.

- Renew your mind with a godly "money" outlook.

- Trust God, not money.

- Prevent money from manipulating you.

- Use money to please God, not man.

- Avoid consuming all your seed (money), or you will have nothing to plant.

- Make regular deposits in God's kingdom.

- Be frugal.

- Save a portion of all the money you receive.

- Put a stop to credit (spending tomorrow's money today).

- Live below your means.

- Spend time planning, budgeting, and controlling your finances. Retire debt, so you are free to give.

- Get to give—then give away all you can.

- Invest in winning souls for Christ.

- Money is your servant. You are not money's servant.

Deposits in the Bank of Heaven

How do you make deposits into your heavenly account? You can deposit in tithes, offerings, and alms.

Tithing is a part of God's covenant of blessing. It is giving back to God 10 percent of everything we have received. The Israelites presented their tithes to the high priest. Our High Priest is Jesus, and our tithes are to be presented to Him.

When we bring our tithes to the Lord, we are blessing Him. Tithing is a spiritual law, and it brings a reward.

Honor the LORD from your wealth, and from the first of all your produce; so your barns will be filled with plenty and your vats will overflow with new wine. (Proverbs 3:9–10)

When we tithe, invest our income with Jesus, God promises to fill our every need; but He has promised us much more than that:

"Bring the whole tithe into the storehouse, so that there may be food in My house, and test Me now in this," says the LORD of hosts, "if I will not open for you the windows of heaven and pour out for you a blessing until it overflows." (Malachi 3:10)

Your blessings won't just trickle down, they will overflow and they will absolutely overwhelm you. Tithing is the first step to investing in your heavenly prosperity account.

Ripped Off or God's Gift?

I know a pastor in Lisbon, Portugal, whose congregation is over 40,000 and his Angolan ministry is over 50,000. Pastor George, also an electrical engineer and architect, built a large church. A week before the first conference in the building, his government declared, "This building does not pass inspection! We are tearing it down!" Bulldozers ripped away until the building was completely demolished. When Pastor George heard the news, did he backslide, rebuke the devil, scream, or hit his wife? George turned to God, "God, I put the best into the church. I thought you had me build it. How did I miss it? Had I known it would be ripped up, I would have used inferior materials."

God replied, "I wanted you to use the best, so I could bless you. Trust me—the 10 percent is your first fruit. The next 90 percent will come easy." George relinquished the ruins as a sacrifice. Acting in response to international human rights pressure, the Portuguese regime paid *double* for the building and *gave him even more land!* Hallelujah!

God promises tithers, *"Bring all the tithes into the storehouse...And I will rebuke the devourer for your sakes, so that he will not destroy the fruit of your ground"* (Malachi 3:10–11 NKJV). Rather than being ripped off, an ugly political act was transformed into God's *gift*—because God was given the best of the first fruits.

Spontaneous Deposits

"Offerings" are the gifts you give when the Holy Spirit nudges you to give above and beyond the tithe. These gifts may be to individuals or to ministries. The Holy Spirit will show you what to give and to whom.

I once needed a wristwatch and I didn't tell anyone. I wanted God to bring it to me. Months went by and still no watch. I just kept praying and claiming the promise in Luke 6:38:

"Give, and it will be given to you. They will pour into your lap a good measure—pressed down, shaken together, and running over."

Tithing

Tithing is a powerful, biblical principle and it can literally change the world.

The Bible lists four rewards of tithing:

1. There will be meat in God's house (enough money to carry on His work).
2. There will not be room enough to receive God's blessings.
3. God will rebuke the destroyer and preserve your wealth.
4. All men will recognize God's blessings.

I reminded the Lord that I had been giving to people around me, people in need. Once I even gave away our grocery money, and now I really needed a watch!

A few days later, just after the holidays, one of our deacons brought his wife over to me and said, "Marilyn, I want you to see a gift that I gave my wife for Christmas." It was a beautiful watch.

I said, "Oh, that's a gorgeous watch!" Then he said, "You know, the Lord has put it on my heart to give you a watch just like that." And I said, "And He's put it on my heart to receive it."

God's law of prosperity says when you give, it will be given back to you. He opens a way for men to give to you. I have given many, many gifts, and I have had all kinds of gifts given to me. It is beautiful to see what God will do for His people, when we understand and follow His statues.

Give to the Poor

God expects us to give tithes. He encourages us to give offerings. Giving to the poor is sowing alms. The Bible says, *"Whoever is kind to a poor man lends to the LORD, and he will reward them for what they have done"* (Proverbs 19:17 NIV). Our gifts to the poor are really gifts to God. They go straight to His heart and cause Him to bless us.

In the Bible, Dorcas was known for giving alms, and was raised from the dead (see Acts 9:36–42), Cornelius was known for his alms-giving, and an angel of God told him, *"Your prayers and alms have ascended as a memorial before God"* (Acts 10:4). Because of his generosity, Cornelius and his household became the first gentiles to receive the baptism of the Holy Spirit (see Acts 10:44–48).

When we give alms, the results are marvelous because sowing is based on the principle of multiplication. You sow one small kernel of corn and it can bring you a whole cornstalk full of ears of corn with thousands of kernels. When you sow alms, you will reap manifold blessings from heaven.

The Dead Sea is an example of something that never gives. I've seen it and believe me, you don't want to swim in it. It has chemicals in it that burn your flesh because the Dead Sea has no outflow. It has a terrible odor, and nothing can grow around it. In order to have God's blessings flowing into us, we must have an outflow or we become like the Dead Sea. Our hearts begin to fill up with toxic waste and our lives really begin to stink!

Withdrawals from Your Account

There are three basic benefits of generous giving:

1. Givers are enriched by God.
2. Receivers have their needs met.
3. God, the ultimate sower of blessings, is praised.

The word "alms" means "mercy." Alms should be given in secret, but you will be rewarded openly. There are many ways to sow alms to the poor. There are alms deeds as well as alms donations; you can volunteer your time as well as your money. Offer to babysit for an overwhelmed single mother in your neighborhood. Make an extra casserole and leave it on the doorstep of an unemployed neighbor. Visit an elderly shut-in or run errands for someone recovering from an illness. Then watch your alms "flow back" to you.

Hilarious Giving

God does not consider the dollar value of your gifts. He is more concerned with the level of your generosity and the attitude with which you give. Jesus watched a widow giving her last two mites. He said:

> *"Truly I say to you, this poor widow put in more than all of*
> *them; for they all out of their surplus put into the offering; but*
> *she out of her poverty put in all that she had to live on."*
> (Luke 21:3–4)

A cheerful giver is a "hilarious giver." When you laugh "hilariously" you hold nothing back—you laugh with your whole being. Your giving is to be the same way.

> *Now this I say, he who sows sparingly will also reap sparingly;*
> *and he who sows bountifully will also reap bountifully.*
> *Each one must do just as he has purposed in his heart, not*
> *grudgingly or under compulsion; for God loves a cheerful*
> *giver.* (2 Corinthians 9:6–7)

Give with every ounce of your heart, with no regrets and no second thoughts and no feeling of obligation. When you give this way, your first reward will be a deep joy in your heart.

In Matthew 20:1–16, there is a parable about a man who hired field hands to bring in his harvest. He hired some people in the morning and promised them a denarius. Then more people came to work at noon, and he promised to give them whatever was right. Late in the day, more people came to work, and he promised them whatever was right, too. At the end of the day, he paid everyone the same amount. The ones that were hired early in the morning complained, "That's not fair. We worked a lot longer. Why did you pay the others the same amount as us?"

The man answered, *"Is your eye envious because I am generous?"* (Matthew 20:15). The generous man here challenged the complainers' thinking. They saw his generosity as being unfair. Their thinking was not generous. Small-mindedness will keep you in darkness.

When you sow generosity, you reap prosperity. This is the law of prosperity which God laid down. God knew when He sowed Jesus—one seed upon the earth—that Jesus would die and bring forth a harvest of many. Now Jesus wants to reward what you sow with a harvest of financial, physical, and spiritual prosperity.

Seven Keys to Prosperity

1. **Be Obedient**
   Therefore keep the words of this covenant and do them, that you may deal wisely and prosper in all that you do. (Deuteronomy 29:9 AMPC)

2. **Put God First**
   "But seek for (aim at and strive after) first of all His kingdom and His righteousness (His way of doing and being right), and then all these things taken together will be given you besides." (Matthew 6:33 AMPC)

3. **Be Diligent in All Things**
   He becomes poor who works with a slack and idle hand, but the hand of the diligent makes rich. (Proverbs 10:4 AMPC)

4. **Use God's Wisdom**
   Riches and honor are with me, enduring wealth and righteousness . . . (Proverbs 8:18 AMPC)

5. **Have a Right Attitude Toward God**
   O taste and see that the LORD is good; how blessed is the man who takes refuge in Him! O fear the LORD, you His saints; for to those who fear Him there is no want. The young lions do lack and suffer hunger; but they who seek the LORD shall not be in want of any good thing. (Psalm 34:8–10)

6. **Meditate on the Word**
   But his delight is in the law of the LORD and in His law he meditates day and night. He will be like a tree firmly planted by streams of water, which yields its fruit in its season, and its leaf does not wither; and in whatever he does, he prospers. (Psalm 1:2–3)

7. **Tithe, Give, and Care for God's House**
   "Bring the whole tithe into the storehouse, so that there may be food in My house, and test Me now in this," says the LORD of hosts, "if I will not open for you the windows of heaven, and pour out for you a blessing until it overflows." (Malachi 3:10)

11/20/23

Is It Godly to Be Poor?

For you know the grace of our Lord Jesus Christ, that though
He was rich, yet for your sake He became poor, so that you
through His poverty might become rich. (2 Corinthians 8:9)

Amen!

Some people think it's a mark of godliness to be poor, or just barely getting along, but that is not God's desire for you. At the wedding feast at Cana, when Mary asked Jesus to make wine for the party, how much wine did He make? Did He make just enough to get by? No, He said, "Pour!" When they poured, they had all that they needed, and more.

Remember when Jesus told the fisherman to let down their nets? They pulled up so many fish that their nets began to tear (see Luke 5:4–6). They did not catch just enough fish to survive. Jesus gave them all the fish they needed and more! When Jesus fed the 5,000, there were 12 baskets of leftovers (see Matthew 14:20)! He did not give them the bare minimum, He gave them an abundance of food.

God is not the God of stinginess; He is the God of generosity. God does not want you to "squeak through." He wants you to be enormously prosperous.

The wedding guests got wine because someone obeyed Jesus's command to pour. The fishermen got fish because they obeyed His command to cast out their nets. The people were fed because the disciples obeyed Jesus's command to set the bread before the 5,000. To receive Christ's abundance in this life, you must be obedient to Him.

Put God First, Then...

Start praising God right now for His provision. Delight in Him and seek Him.

> *"But seek first His kingdom and His righteousness, and all these things shall be added to you."* (Matthew 6:33)

As you read your Bible, ask Him for the wisdom to see His way of doing things. Get in line with His heart and walk with Him in everything you do.

> *For the LORD God is a sun and shield; the LORD gives grace and glory; no good thing does He withhold from those who walk uprightly.* (Psalm 84:11)

To lay claim to the riches which God has stored up for you—you must surrender your worldly motivations for wanting wealth. Put God first: trusting, following, and obeying Him.

Our priority is to keep our eyes on God, alert and ready to bind the devil and his forces in the name of Jesus. Satan is a thief, and he will try to steal your prosperity with seeds of doubt and despair. Bind the devil and say, "You are not going to take away my prosperity!" Loose the forces of heaven to conquer Satan and bring in that prosperity.

> *Are they not all ministering spirits, sent out to render service for the sake of those who will inherit salvation?* (Hebrews 1:14)

Why Money?

Why does God want you to have wealth? God prospers you because He takes pleasure in doing so, but also so you can be a financial blessing to others. God uses our hands to do His work on Earth. Therefore, if He is going to bless a person, He is most likely to use another person to do so. We can become conduits for the riches of God. With His wealth we can establish His covenant. Money is not to fulfill our lust for riches; it's to fulfill His purpose.

We receive, and then we give to the work of God and to others. Then we receive back—probably through people—and have enough to give again. Jesus said, *"Freely you received, freely give"* (Matthew 10:8).

From Financial Prison to Palace Prosperity

It's not *getting* that makes prosperity worth having. It's *giving* that makes prosperity worth getting. Did God prosper Joseph so he could drive the Mercedes of his day—a golden chariot? God took Joseph from the prison to a palace to preserve the lives of his family, the bloodline through which man's salvation—the Messiah—would come. Prosperity fulfills God's priority to win souls.

There are those who say that money is the "root of evil," but this is not true. Money is not itself the root of evil; it is the "love of money" (see 1 Timothy 6:10). Satan will try to show you how to get money or try to convince you to hold on to it, to love it, to be miserly with it. Be sure that it is the Lord you are loving and not money. Do you want wealth for your own worldly satisfaction, or do you want it for the advancement of God's purposes?

Pride can keep you from getting and keeping the wealth that God has for you. Beware of thinking that you prosper due to your own goodness.

> *"Do not say in your heart when the LORD your God has driven them out before you, 'Because of my righteousness the LORD has brought me in to possess this land,' but it is because of the wickedness of these nations that the LORD is dispossessing them before you. Know, then, it is not because of your righteousness that the LORD your God is giving you this good land to possess, for you are a stubborn people."* (Deuteronomy 9:4, 6)

Always remember, give credit where it's due.

> *But you shall remember the LORD your God, for it is He who is giving you power to make wealth, that He may confirm His covenant which He swore to your fathers, as it is this day.* (Deuteronomy 8:18)

True prosperity comes not from your efforts but from God's generosity, and God-given prosperity is to be used to advance His kingdom.

Renewing Your Mind

God doesn't want to prosper you just materially or financially; more importantly, He wants to prosper your soul (see 3 John 2). Jerry Savelle writes in *Prosperity of the Soul*, "A prosperous soul is one in which the mind is renewed, the will conformed, the emotions controlled, and the thinking faculties selective of that which it thinks." A prosperous soul encompasses your entire being—the "real you" inside your body. Without a prospering soul, material wealth will be fleeting.

The best way to renew your mind is to replace your thoughts with God's. His thoughts are much higher than yours, and more effective. When God made you a new creature, He gave you Christ's mind.

> *... But we have the mind of Christ (the Messiah) and do hold the thoughts (feelings and purposes) of His heart.*
> (1 Corinthians 2:16 AMPC)

The way to experience the mind of Christ is to flood your mind with His Word! We are commanded to "renew" our mind. When we do, our souls will prosper!

> *"For My thoughts are not your thoughts. Nor are your ways My ways," declares the LORD. "For as the heavens are higher than the earth, so are My ways higher than your ways and My thoughts than your thoughts."* (Isaiah 55:8–9)

You are constantly making choices. You can decide to do things your way, the world's way, or God's way. You face hundreds of decisions each day. Everything you do is a choice. You can even choose not to choose! With each choice you make, ask yourself this question: "Is this choice conformed to God's will?"

And do not be conformed to this world, but be transformed by the renewing of your mind, so that you may prove what the will of God is, that which is good and acceptable and perfect. (Romans 12:2)

If this goal seems overwhelming, remember that God will enable you to do His will: *"It is God who is at work in you, both to will and to work for His good pleasure"* (Philippians 2:13). He gives you the desire to conform to His will. Yield to Him and prosper your soul!

There are times when emotions seem to rule your life. Satan loves to have fear, anxiety, anger, or worry control you. If emotions are dictating your choices, then emotions have taken the driver's seat of your soul. When this happens, your actions will be unproductive—not prosperous. You can claim the strength of Christ and regain control of your will.

You already have all the right qualities inside you, through Christ. It is a matter of switching control from your emotions to His emotions which are called the fruit of the Spirit.

But the fruit of the Spirit is love, joy, peace, patience, kindness, goodness, faithfulness, gentleness, self-control; against such things there is no law. (Galatians 5:22–23)

The fruit of the Spirit is available through the presence of the Holy Spirit in our lives! Look at that list again—the possessor of those qualities is a prosperous soul!

When your soul prospers, you walk in the wisdom of the Lord, thinking His kind of thoughts, living by His kind of faith. Conform your will to His by making the quality decision to choose God's ways. Control your emotions by remembering that Jesus is the source for everything you need in your life. His Spirit has positive emotional fruit for every negative feeling that comes your way.

Promises

Read these Old Testament promises to strengthen your faith!

Exodus 15:26	Psalm 103:2–3
Deuteronomy 7:15	Isaiah 19:22
Deuteronomy 32:39	Isaiah 57:18–19
2 Kings 20:5–6	Jeremiah 30:17
Job 5:18	Jeremiah 33:6
Psalm 30:2	Hosea 6:1
Psalm 91:10	

Physical Prosperity

Walk in the Word in every area of your life! Some people say, "I believe I'm to prosper spiritually," but they have not learned that God also wants them to prosper physically. Their attitude is not in alignment with God's Word. How could a God, Who is the source of all prosperity, prosper us in our finances and souls but not in our bodies?

Beloved, I pray that in all respects you may prosper and be in good health, just as your soul prospers. (3 John 2, emphasis added)

Our health was part of the reason Jesus came to Earth: "*HE HIMSELF TOOK OUT INFIRMITIES, AND CARRIED AWAY OUR DISEASES*" (Matthew 8:17). When Jesus went about preaching, He looked at the bodies of people as well as their souls. He was concerned with the prosperity of the whole person. Whenever He preached the gospel, He also healed the sick and delivered the mentally tormented.

God reveals in His Word that He wants us to be healthy. He never said that we should bear up under sickness with a grim and determined patience. Jesus healed sickness whenever there was faith present. His Word instructs us to ask for healing (see James 5:14). You are to prosper in health until the day you go home: "*As your days, so shall your strength be*" (Deuteronomy 33:25 NKJV).

Until you learn to prosper and allow God to be glorified in your life, you will never know the great things He has in store for you. The key to receiving God's prosperity is *perseverance.* You cannot afford to get discouraged.

We count those blessed who endured. You have heard of the endurance of Job and have seen the outcome of the Lord's dealings, that the Lord is full of compassion and is merciful. (James 5:11)

The next time you feel like you are losing everything, remember how things turned out for Job. If you are suffering sickness or hardship, put your faith in Christ, and you will be healed and receive double what you lost. God promised to supply your needs according to His riches—that is a bountiful supply!

GOD HAS GIVEN YOU THE POWER TO MAKE WEALTH.

STEPS TO BELIEVING BIG

1.

Meditate on the "Seven Keys to Prosperity" found on page 245 and the accompanying verses. Write out what you can do to receive God's blessings.

_____

_____

_____

_____

_____

_____

_____

2.

Read about the fruit of the Spirit in Galatians 5:22–23. Think of ways you can share God's emotions (rather than your own) with an unsaved loved one or friend.

3.

Using the scriptures listed below, compare and contrast how one's attitude toward riches affects prosperity.

Matthew 6:19–24, 25:40–45

_____

_____

Luke 6:38, 12:15

_____
_____
_____
_____

Corinthians 9:6–10

_____
_____
_____
_____

4.

Pray for financial wisdom. Ask God where you can cheerfully invest in His kingdom and whom you should bless financially.

5.

Where do you need healing? Memorize one of the following verses to remind you that God heals all aspects of your life:

Psalm 103:2–3

Isaiah 61:1

Jeremiah 3:22, 30:17

Hosea 6:1

Malachi 4:2

12

FAITH THAT CHANGES
HEARTS AND MINDS

*I urge, then, first of all, that petitions, prayers, intercession
and thanksgiving be made for all people—for kings and all
those in authority, that we may live peaceful and quiet lives
in all godliness and holiness. This is good, and pleases God
our Savior, who wants all people to be saved and to come to a
knowledge of the truth. (1 Timothy 2:1–4 NIV)*

Can you pray with faith knowing that a person's will is opposed to the answer? Your prayers will many times be in direct contrast to another's will in a situation. You may pray for the restoration of a marriage when one or the other partner seems set on giving it up and going into another relationship. You may pray for the restoration of a rebellious child when he/she is making decisions contrary to God's Word, living out of God's will, and consistently telling you that he/she does not want to follow God. Can you pray with faith for God to change the person's will?

Someone you love very much may be against the baptism of the Holy Spirit and even teach contrary to what you believe. You may be praying in faith for them to receive the baptism of the Holy Spirit, but they are not willing. Will God answer your prayer?

Often, when we are praying for something that is against someone else's will, we say, "Well, I prayed in faith; now it is up to that individual and God, my part is over." If your prayer is not answered, you can easily blame it on another's unwillingness to yield to God—they had a free will in the situation and chose to go against God—but is this really the way God works?

God Works How?

When Christ was resurrected, God gave Him a name above every name, seated Him at His right hand, and put all things under His feet. All authority was given to Him.

> *Which He brought about in Christ, when He raised Him from the dead and seated Him at His right hand in the heavenly places, far above all rule and authority and power and dominion, and every name that is named, not only in this age but also in the one to come. And He put all things in subjection under His feet, and gave Him as head over all things to the church, which is His body, the fullness of Him who fills all in all.* (Ephesians 1:20–23)

Jesus then transferred His authority to His church. He gave us

His name as "power of attorney" to do His will on earth. We are to act as His representatives, in His name. Just before Jesus left this earth, He said:

> *"All authority has been given to Me in heaven and on earth. Go therefore and make disciples of all the nations, baptizing them in the name of the Father and the Son and the Holy Spirit, teaching them to observe all that I commanded you; and lo, I am with you always, even to the end of the age."* (Matthew 28:18–20)

Jesus gave His authority to the church. Jesus came with authority and sends us out in His authority. He said to the Father, "As You have sent me, so send I them into the world" (see John 17:18). Jesus is seated in heaven, but He is working down here through His body, the church. God has been clear in His Word as to what His will is. He has given the church the authority and power to do His will. Now He waits for the church to do her part.

Persistent Pretender

We, as the body of Christ, cannot function without the Head— Christ. However, what we sometimes do not understand is that the Head has chosen to work through the church. The Word says that the branches cannot bear fruit unless they are attached to the vine, and yet the vine without the branches cannot bear fruit either. God is using you and others of the body of Christ to accomplish His work on earth.

We are to bind and loose on earth what was bound and loosed

in heaven. When Jesus stripped Satan, He bound Satan's authority over you.

> *"I will give you the keys of the kingdom of heaven; and whatever you shall bind on earth shall have been bound in heaven, and whatever you loose on earth shall have been loosed in heaven."* (Matthew 16:19)

Jesus gave us authority to loose the Spirit and bind up Satan on earth.

The problem is that Satan pretends that he didn't get the message and proceeds with guerrilla warfare against the saints. Satan has no *legal right* to attack us, but will render us useless if we allow him to; yet, Jesus said that the gates of hell will not prevail against us. Instead of Satan taking over our territory, we are to take over his.

God Promises to Answer

Some years ago, people would say to me, "If you're praying for someone to be saved, you have to always remember that every person has a will and you can't overcome someone's will." I got into a pattern of looking at the Word and then looking at the person's will. When I looked at their will, it wasn't a very happy circumstance, because they really didn't want to serve the Lord. I was putting their will above the power of God.

Before Wally and I were married, I asked him if he felt "called" into the ministry, because I did not want to marry a minister. He assured me that he did not feel called at all. I said, "I do not ever want to be in the ministry," and he answered, "No, don't worry about it, I'll never go into the ministry." About three years a.. we got married, Wally began to come home every weekend, and say, "Oh, I feel called into the ministry." His will was being changed by God.

You may be saying, "I'll never serve God full-time," but don't count on it. If God has called you, He knows how to get through to you. Today, I am in the ministry, and I've never been happier in my life. I was as rebellious as anyone, but there were people praying and standing on the Word for me, and my thoughts began to come into obedience to the Lord Jesus Christ.

Is Your Request Sincere?

Matthew 7:7–8 says, *"Ask, and it will be given to you; seek, and you will find; knock, and it will be opened to you. For everyone who asks receives, and he who seeks finds, and to him who knocks it will be opened."*

The word used here for "ask" means:
• To beg • To call for • To crave • To desire • To require

When you pray for a rebellious will to change, it must be more than a wimpy little request. Be passionate! Crave the salvation of a rebel, beg for it, desire it with all your heart.

You Have Power

Where do you get the strength and authority to order the devil around? Although the demoniac of Gadara was possessed by a legion of spirits, they could not stop him from running to Jesus. Christ has power over every demon.

> *"And these signs will accompany those who believe: In my name they will drive out demons; they will speak in new tongues; they will pick up snakes with their hands; and when they drink deadly poison, it will not hurt them at all; they will place their hands on sick people, and they will get well."* (Mark 16:17–18 NIV)

Jesus has given you the same authority. On this earth, believers have been assigned to bind the forces of evil and loose the love of God. As part of the Lord's body, you have both the authority and the power to walk on the enemy.

You Have Weapons

Changing the will of another cannot be done by scheming, plotting, or manipulation. This is a spiritual battle and our commanding general has provided us with the most effective spiritual weapons. Although we lead natural lives, the battle we are fighting is spiritual.

> *For though we walk in the flesh, we do not war according to the flesh, for the weapons of our warfare are not of the flesh, but divinely powerful for the destruction of fortresses. We are destroying speculations and every lofty thing raised up against the knowledge of God, and we are taking every thought captive to the obedience of Christ.* (2 Corinthians 10:3–5)

Many times, we mistakenly fight with human, emotional, and psychological weapons. These do not work, and we think that God has refused our prayers. That is not the case. We have argued, tried to convince, maybe even coerced someone to listen to our message. Instead, we needed to bind the enemy, intercede in faith, prepare the soil of their hearts for the good seed, then plant the Word. The Lord will cause the seed to grow.

What's In A Name?

What does it mean to pray in the name of Jesus? The Greek word for "name" in the Bible covers everything, including the thought or feeling which is aroused in the mind by mentioning, hearing, or remembering the person's name.

When you pray in His name, be sure that your heart and mind are dwelling on everything that Jesus means to you (the relationship you share with Him, and every memory you have of His working in your life). Praying in His name is praying, not just with your mouth, but with your entire being.

Whale Songs

Sometimes we pray in faith and trust God to change the will of a rebellious loved one, but nothing happens. This will really test your faith. When doubts start creeping in, you may be tempted to make plans of your own. When you are getting impatient in your petitions and are ready to give up, look at some of the marvelous examples of how God works on the wills of rebels.

Jonah was determined to run away from God (see the book of Jonah). His will was set. God was also determined to give the city of Nineveh a chance to repent. He gave Jonah the command to go and preach repentance. Jonah refused and went the other direction. One of God's ways to deal with His servants is to make it difficult to disobey. He let Jonah see the result of his rebellion. Thrown overboard and swallowed by a large fish, Jonah developed a whole different attitude.

God has plenty more whales from where that one came, enough for all the rebels that you know. Look at what happened next: Jonah repented, went to Nineveh and preached, and there was a mighty revival there! If Jonah had never gone, thousands of rebels would have been lost. If you don't do what God tells you to do, who could be lost? How many families would never know Jesus? How many people might never be healed because you gave up too soon.

Some time back, Wally and I were at a special occasion where most of the people there were unsaved. The dinner was for a young couple, and the young man had just received Christ. He was on fire for Christ! He was seated beside his unsaved brother, and the brother offered him a cigarette. He replied, "No, thanks, I don't smoke." The brother was surprised, because this young man had always smoked. So, the brother asked, "Why did you just suddenly stop?" This wonderful young man said, "I had orders from above."

Later at this same dinner, the young man's father listened to the gospel with an open heart and was almost ready to pray the sinner's prayer. This young man, newly born again, was bringing light to his entire household, and I believe that entire family will come to Jesus.

Rebel with a Dark Cause

Let's look at another rebel, one who killed Christians just because they were Christians. Saul of Tarsus thought that he was doing his duty to God by persecuting Christians. He was sincere, but he was sincerely wrong. Saul was doing the devil's work, because the devil is a murderer. Somebody probably came against the forces of darkness that influenced Saul's will. One of those praying may have been Stephen, because when Stephen was dying, Saul was standing there watching. Stephen prayed as he was dying, *"Lord, do not hold this sin against them!"* (Acts 7:60).

When Saul was on his way to Damascus, a light hit him, and Saul became a devoted servant of Jesus Christ. With a new will and a new name, Paul became the greatest evangelist of the early church, and even wrote two-thirds of the New Testament. What happened to his will? His will got in line with the wisdom from above, and through him, God changed the world.

He Changed You, Didn't He?

We were all rebels against the Lord, but He drew us, brought us to the cross, and made us new creatures. Think back to the time before you were born again. Weren't you a rebel making decisions with the wisdom of the world? Someone interceded for you (you may not even know your intercessor personally) and your will was changed. If He changed us, is there anyone He cannot change? Jesus said, "all things are possible with God" (see Matthew 19:26)

> *The [Holy] Spirit and the bride (the Church, the true*
> *Christians) say, Come! And let him who is listening say,*
> *Come! And let everyone come who is thirsty [who is painfully*
> *conscious of his need of those things by which the soul*
> *is refreshed, supported and strengthened]; and whoever*
> *[earnestly] desires to do it, let him come, take, appropriate,*
> *and drink the water of life without cost.*
> (Revelation 22:17 AMPC)

Now it is time for you to intercede for someone. It takes both the Spirit and the bride to give the invitation for salvation. You are part of the bride. The Father has chosen to use the bride, as well as the Spirit, to give the invitation.

Watch out for the "Word thief." As you intercede for the unsaved, the Father of Lies just gets more and more irritated. He doesn't want those souls saved. He will whisper lies in your ear to discourage your faith and encourage doubt. He will try to steal your harvest. He hopes that worldly cares and worldly wisdom will cause your harvest to rot in the fields.

The Heart of a King

God can change the will of someone who is not a Christian. He can also change the will of a rebellious Christian. Can we change the will of leaders of nations, people who don't even know God? Yes, we can with God's help. The Bible says that the hearts of kings are in the hands of God, *"The king's heart is like channels of water in the hand of the Lord; He turns it wherever He wishes"* (Proverbs 21:1). We must come against evil spirits that are over nations, and over leaders of nations. As we come against those strongholds, God can take the hearts and turn them the way they should go to bless that nation.

Kings Who Bowed to God's Will

- Ahasuerus/Artaxerxes (Esther 6; Nehemiah 2)
- Nebuchadnezzar (Ezekiel 29:18–19; Daniel 4)
- Cyrus (Ezra 1:1; Isaiah 44:28)
- Darius (Ezra 6:22)
- Augustus (Luke 2:1–7)

In the time of Ezra, the Israelites were returning to Israel. They were to rebuild their city and their temple, but they had no money. They prayed and God touched the heart of the Persian king, who then passed a decree allowing all Jews to go home. He also gave them money to rebuild the temple.

Such a thing can only happen when people behind the scenes pray and bind the rulers of darkness. We have great power and authority, even over entire nations.

Two Information Networks

Men listen to one of two sources of wisdom and information: God or the devil. James 3:13–18 tells us about two kinds of wisdom. There is a wisdom that is earthly, sensual, and demonic—the wisdom of this world. The wisdom of the world brings bitterness, envy, strife, and confusion. It eventually produces death, fear, and a host of bad results. The *"wisdom from above"* (v. 17), on the other hand, is pure, peaceable, and gentle and it produces life and faith.

Our job is to decide which kind of wisdom motivates our wills. God wants to draw all men to Himself; He wants everyone to come to repentance. However, there is a hindering force, a spirit that will snatch God's Word from hearts and bring confusion and blindness to their minds.

Men and women who are not walking with Jesus draw from worldly wisdom. They don't know about the pure, gentle, heavenly wisdom. Their decisions are made with earthly wisdom which controls their wills.

> *In whose case the god of this world has blinded the minds*
> *of the unbelieving so that they might not see the light of the*
> *gospel of the glory of Christ, who is the image of God.*
> (2 Corinthians 4:4)

Romans 7:14–25 describes a man who is doing things contrary to his will. He is in a constant war, *"... practicing what I would like to do, but I am doing the very thing that I hate"* (v. 15). It is a war of the flesh versus the spirit.

There are many people who are in this state. In their innermost being they want to serve the Lord, but they are bound. Praise God there is an answer! Jesus Christ has set us free from the authority of sin in our lives—the influence that would keep us doing what we do not want to do. Christ set us free from the evil influences within and outside us that would govern our wills. We need to declare that freedom and pray that people will see their choice to be free.

Forget "Plan B"

Many times, we pray with what we call *faith,* but all the time we are making alternate plans—in case God does not come through with an answer. That is what the Bible calls "double-mindedness." If we do not know God's will on a matter, then we pray for wisdom, guidance, and clear counsel. When we know God's revealed will, we can pray without hesitation, without doubt, and in complete faith, knowing that we will receive our petition. Jesus said, *"Ask, and it will be given to you . . . "* (Matthew 7:7, emphasis added).

Faith is agreeing with God's Word concerning a need and then acting like it will actually happen. God said He would answer the prayer of faith. Is your prayer of faith conditional? The Word says that if you believe, you *will* receive.

Jesus said that we are light and salt to this world:

> *"You are the salt of the earth; but if the salt has become tasteless, how can it be made salty again? It is no longer good for anything, except to be thrown out and trampled under foot by men."You are the light of the world. A city set on a hill cannot be hidden."* (Matthew 5:13–14)

Light causes the darkness to flee. It does not have a choice. Salt is a preservative and overcomes the tendency to disintegrate and decay. We, as the *"salt of the earth,"* are to overcome the decay of the world. The world would already have destroyed itself because of its filth and rottenness if it were not for the salt of the earth. We are hindering that destruction because of the nature of God in us.

Since our source of light is God, we will continue to shine regardless of the way those who *"sit in darkness"* respond. Our light source, God, is inextinguishable! It is our faith that overcomes the world—regardless of what the world wills or thinks! We don't need an alternate plan. "Plan A" is perfect!

Are You Helping God?

Do you think God is too slow in answering your prayers for another's salvation? When we care for someone, we are tempted to get impatient and take things into our own hands. Let the *"Lord of the harvest"* (Matthew 9:38) decide when harvest time has come.

Don't give up on prayer and faith! If you set a certain date for someone to get saved and turn their life over to God, you may be tempted to give up if it doesn't happen according to your deadline. God does not want you to give up; therefore, do not set a time for your harvest and don't quit praying! Keep planting the seed, using your weapons, and interceding until God's time comes, and "your rebel" is in the body of Christ.

Don't try to help God with His master plan. We may try to bribe our loved one: offer Sunday dinner of all their favorite foods if they'll just come to church. We may try to use guilt on Mother's Day by saying, "Go to church one time before your grandma dies— it would make her so happy." We are trying to use natural methods to fight a spiritual battle—it won't work!

We are human, but we can't wage a spiritual war with *human* methods. Rather, we must use God's mighty weapons to knock down the devil's strongholds. With these weapons we conquer their rebellious ideas and teach them to obey Christ. You cannot change another's will through your own actions. Our job is to bring the unsaved and the rebellious before God in prayer.

It is not your *effort* that brings answered prayer. You cannot use your will to overcome the will of another. Do not allow yourself to become weary and tired, continuing in your own strength. *It is the power of God that will break down the strongholds.* Using His power does not require yours. Depend upon and trust that your God and His Word will do the work, not your methods. Let God deal with another's free will. Faithfully perform the task God gave to you and trust Him to honor His Word. He knows how to handle people.

Resting in God

Remember that your faith is in God and in His Word. When you have been faithful in intercession for another, then rest. Trust God to do His Work. If, on occasion, a person's will has not changed, leave that to God, too. God loves that person more than you do and knows exactly how to deal with them. If you have unanswered questions in a situation, remember Deuteronomy 29:29:

> *"The secret things belong to the LORD our God, but the things revealed belong to us and to our sons forever, that we may observe all the words of this law."*

Your task is to act on the "revealed" things and trust God with those things that you don't understand.

STEPS TO BELIEVING BIG

1.

List some signs that might reveal one's rebellion against God's will. Ask God to show you if you have any of these characteristics in your life.

_____
_____
_____
_____
_____

2.

Find five examples from the Bible of rebellious wills being changed. Write down these verses.

_____
_____
_____
_____
_____
_____
_____
_____

3.

Meditate on James 3:1–18 from your Bible. Write out
the two kinds of wisdom men can receive. Choose
one nation whose ruler is not acting in the wisdom of
God. Resolve to intercede for this ruler and nation.

_____

_____

_____

_____

_____

4.

Study this last chapter and find some faith confessions
you can use to pray for unsaved relatives and friends.

_____

_____

_____

_____

_____

5.

Starting today, be especially alert to messages of
worldly wisdom (in the media, at the office, in
conversations with friends). Ask God to bring His light
of truth to the dark world of counterfeit wisdom.

MARILYN HICKEY

Encouraging, optimistic, always upbeat, and energetic, Marilyn Hickey actively ministers around the world to fulfill her calling to *cover the earth with the Word.* As founder and president of *Marilyn Hickey Ministries*, a non-profit ministry and humanitarian organization based in Denver, Colorado, Marilyn has impacted many countries worldwide: from disaster relief efforts in Haiti, Indonesia, and Pakistan to providing food for the hungry in Mexico, Costa Rica, Russia, and the Philippines.

Her legacy also includes significant visits to Islamic countries. In 2016, more than one million people attended her meeting in Karachi, Pakistan, and in 2019 she was selected by Pakistani President, Arif Aivi, and Grand Imam, Maulana Syed Muhammad Abdul Khabir Azad, to receive an International Lifetime Peace Award.

Marilyn has traveled to 137 countries and has had audiences with government leaders and heads of state all over the globe. She was the first woman to join the board of directors for Dr. David Yonggi Cho (Pastor of the world's largest congregation, Yoido Full Gospel Church in South Korea).

She co-hosts a daily, globally-broadcasted television program, *Today with Marilyn & Sarah*, along with her daughter, Pastor Sarah Bowling. *Today with Marilyn & Sarah* is shown in over 100 countries with a potential viewing audience of 2.5 billion households worldwide.

Marilyn has authored over 100 publications; including her autobiography, *It's Not Over Until You Win.*

She and her late husband Wallace were married over 50 years, and have two children and four grandchildren. Marilyn holds the following degrees of education: Bachelor of Arts in Collective Foreign Languages from the University of Northern Colorado and an Honorary Doctorate of Divinity degree from Oral Roberts University.

In 2015, Marilyn was honored at Oral Roberts University with the prestigious Lifetime Global Achievement Award. This award recognizes individuals or organizations that have made a significant impact in the history of ORU and in the world in positive ways as an extension of the university and its mission. Marilyn's greatest passion and desire is to continue being a bridge builder in countries around the world, and she shows no signs of stopping.

NOTES

CHAPTER 1

Page 3   *Faith is…: Merriam-Webster, s.v. "Faith (n.)," accessed August 3, 2020, https://www.merriam-webster.com/dictionary/faith.*

Page 5   *In his book…: David Yonggi Cho, The Fourth Dimension (Alachua: Bridge-Logos, combined edition, 2016), 1.*

Page 5   *Page 5 Sitting on eggs…: Merriam-Webster, s.v. "Incubate (v.)," accessed August 3, 2020, https://www.merriam-webster.com/ dictionary/incubate.*

Page 5   *First, visualize a…: Yonggi Cho, The Fourth Dimension, 1–12.*

Page 6   *Second, you must…: Yonggi Cho, The Fourth Dimension, 12–13.*

Page 6   *Third, pray for…: Yonggi Cho, The Fourth Dimension, 13–16.*

Page 6   *Finally, speak the…: Yonggi Cho, The Fourth Dimension, 16–21.*

CHAPTER 2

Page 28   *The Inner Journey of Faith…: W. E. Vine, Vine's Complete Expository Dictionary of Old and New Testament Words (Nashville: Nelson, 1997), 563.*

Page 30   *Logos…: Vine, Vine's Complete Expository Dictionary of Old and New Testament Words, 1241-1242.*

Page 30   *Rhema…: Vine, Vine's Complete Expository Dictionary of Old and New Testament Words, 1242.*

Page 30   *The word redeem…: Merriam-Webster, s.v. "Redeem (v.)," accessed August 3, 2020, https://www.merriam-webster.com/ dictionary/reedem.*

Page 37   *First, let's be clear…: Vine, Vine's Complete Expository Dictionary of Old and New Testament Words, 727.*

CHAPTER 3

Page 55 *A gossip is…: Merriam-Webster, s.v.* "Gossip (*n.*)," accessed August 3, 2020, https://www.merriam-webster.com/dictionary/gossip.

Page 61 *Edify…:* Vine, *Vine's Complete Expository Dictionary of Old and New Testament Words,* 347-348.

Page 70 *Practice…: Merriam-Webster, s.v.* "Practice (*v.*)," accessed August 3, 2020, https://www.merriam-webster.com/dictionary/practice.

CHAPTER 4

Page 78 *Timnath-serah:* "Timnath-serah," *Abarim Publications,* accessed August 3, 2020, https://www.abarim-publications.com/Meaning/Timnath-serah.html#.XyhYSK-Sm70.

Page 85 *Medical research shows…:* Yonggi Cho, *The Fourth Dimension,* 47-49.

Page 88 *Nelson's Illustrated…:* Ronald F. Youngblood, F. F. Bruce, and R. K. Harrison, *Nelson's New Illustrated Bible Dictionary* (Nashville: Nelson, 1995), 264.

Page 88 *We maintain…:* Kenneth Copeland, *Prayer: Your Foundation for Success* (Shippensburg: Harrison, 2012), 13-14.

Page 88 *Since God cannot…:* Don Gossett, *What You Say Is What You Get!* (Springdale: Whitaker, 1976).

CHAPTER 5

Page 96 *The word fear…:* Vine, *Vine's Complete Expository Dictionary of Old and New Testament Words,* 414.

Page 97 *Deilia, which means…:* Vine, *Vine's Complete Expository Dictionary of Old and New Testament Words,* 414-415.

Page 97 *The root word pachad…:* "6343. Pachad" *Bible Hub,* accessed August 5, 2020, https://biblehub.com/hebrew/6343.htm.

Page 98 *Eulabeia…:* Vine, *Vine's Complete Expository Dictionary of Old and New Testament Words*, 415.

CHAPTER 6

Page 121 *Learn to endure…: Merriam-Webster, s.v.* "Endure (*v.*)," accessed August 3, 2020, https://www.merriam-webster.com/dictionary/endure.

Page 122 *Tsarap:* James Strong, *The New Strong's Complete Dictionary of Bible Words* (Nashville: Nelson, 1996), 504.

Page 122 *Peirazo:* Strong, *The New Strong's Complete Dictionary of Bible Words*, 678.

Page 122 *Nacah:* Strong, *The New Strong's Complete Dictionary of Bible Words*, 454.

Page 123 *Stronghold:* Strong, *The New Strong's Complete Dictionary of Bible Words*, 672.

CHAPTER 7

Page 142 *Hebrew word kabash…:* Strong, *The New Strong's Complete Dictionary of Bible Words*, 400.

Page 145 *Exousia:* Strong, *The New Strong's Complete Dictionary of Bible Words*, 618.

Page 145 *Toqeph:* Strong, *The New Strong's Complete Dictionary of Bible Words*, 558.

Page 152 *Sin, defined as…:* Strong, *The New Strong's Complete Dictionary of Bible Words*, 574.

CHAPTER 8

Page 173   *Bartimaeus means…:* Strong, *The New Strong's Complete Dictionary of Bible Words*, 21.

CHAPTER 9

Page 192   *Methuselah's name is…:* "Methuselah," *Abarim Publications*, accessed August 5, 2020, https://www.abarim-publications. com/Meaning/Methuselah.html#.XyrsNK-Sm70.

Page 195   *He was called Abram…:* "Abram," *Abarim Publications*, accessed August 5, 2020, https://www.abarim-publications. com/Meaning/Abram.html#.Xyrt26-Sm70.

Page 195   *First called Abram…:* Strong, *The New Strong's Complete Dictionary of Bible Words*, 2.

Page 197   *Amram means…:* "Amram," *Abarim Publications*, accessed August 5, 2020, https://www.abarim-publications.com/ Meaning/Amram.html#.Xyrtk6-Sm70.

Page 197   *Jochebed means…:* Strong, *The New Strong's Complete Dictionary of Bible Words*, 141.

CHAPTER 10

Page 208   *He is Jehovah-Shammah…:* "Jehovah-Shammah," *Bible Hub*, accessed August 5, 2020, https://biblehub.com/ topical/j/jehovah-shammah.htm.

Page 209   *Hebrew word halak…:* Strong, *The New Strong's Complete Dictionary of Bible Words*, 353.

CHAPTER 11

Page 242   *The word alms…:* Strong, *The New Strong's Complete Dictionary of Bible Words,* 613.

Page 250   *Prosperity of the Soul…:* Jerry Savelle, *Prosperity of the Soul* (Shippensburg: Harrison, 1979).

CHAPTER 12

Page 263   *The word used here for ask means…:* Strong, *The New Strong's Complete Dictionary of Bible Words,* 571.

NOTES

NOTES

NOTES

NOTES

NOTES

NOTES

NOTES

NOTES

NOTES

_____

_____

_____

_____

_____

_____

_____

_____

_____

_____

_____

_____

_____

_____

_____

_____

_____

_____

_____

NOTES